With my best wishes

Jim Klobuchar

Walking Briskly
Toward the
Sunset

Walking Briskly Toward the Sunset

by

Jim Klobuchar

NODIN PRESS

Acknowledgements

The author wishes to thank a number of publishers and editors for permission to reprint in this book portions of his writings that appear in prior publications. These include the *Christian Science Monitor*; the University of Minnesota Press, publisher of *Minstrel* in which his stories dealing with Ginger Rogers and his early years in northern Minnesota first appeared; Weldon Owen of San Francisco, publisher of *Over Minnesota*, in which his brief description of Minnesota's wolf country first appeared; Adventure Publications of Cambridge, MN., in which some of his writings on pro football first appeared in *The Knights and Knaves of Autumn*; Kirk House Publishing of Edina, MN., publisher of the author's *The Cross Under the Acacia Tree* and *The Miracles of Barefoot Capitalism*; and the National Football League Publication *Game Day*, in which the author's eulogy of Walter Payton first appeared.

Most of the rest of the material in this book was written for the author's two websites, **http://www.jimklobuchar.com** and **http://www.jimklobucharwrites**, or is material intended for future publication.

The cover photo depicting a scene above the Big Sur in California is by the author's wife, Susan Cornell Wilkes.

The author also wishes to thank Norton Stillman and John Toren of Nodin Press for their interest in this book and contributions to it.

ISBN 1-932472-37-1

Designed and edited by John Toren
Nodin Press is a division of Micawber's, Inc.
530 N. Third Street, Suite 120
Minneapolis, MN 55401

This is for Amy and Meagan, who will remember the Tetons and the unprovoked attack on our tent by a surly porcupine when you were children; and I hope you will never forget the wonder of Lake Solitude at sunrise on your first walk in the mountains.

Photo Credits

Table of Contents

Iv. Africa Spins The Mind

V. Life in Today's Arena: Helmets and Stock Options

VI. The World Begins a New Millennium and the Road to Sanity Narrows

PREFACE

The Muted Joy of a Sunset

What you will find in this book are some of the stories and musings that escaped through the cracks of retirement after one man's career in daily journalism—forty-three years of it. Originally I schemed a retirement of relative serenity. I thought of a month in the Rocky Mountains, another in Switzerland, a refresher course in a Trappist monastery or an off-the-wall project of learning how to understand women.

Nothing much of this happened.

I didn't realize at the time that writing and reporting over such a span of time can become a pathological condition, more or less beyond the reach of conventional medicine.

No such thoughts occupied my mind on a December night eight years ago when I walked through the city room for the last time. As usual, the night staff of the *Minneapolis Star Tribune* was absorbed in the early stages of organizing the next day's newspaper. I was weighed down with collectibles from my emptied desk and by the lump in my throat.

I don't know what appearance I made that evening but *somber* wouldn't have been a bad guess. After nearly a half century of fulltime journalism, mostly print, some in broadcast, I looked at the faces I'd known so long and tried to smile and nod. It wasn't exactly an epic recessional. In earlier times the city room's typewriters might have been mistaken for an army of crickets noising their way through the night, but that night it was quiet, like every night since the electronic revolution changed newspapering forever. Fingers tapping on computer keyboards don't create much din. Phones don't jangle any more. The chaotic melodrama of my early years had long since yielded to a kind of sanitized orderliness. Nobody yells "Copy!" and the cloud banks of cigarette smoke had been sucked up years ago by common sense and the pronouncements from the surgeon general's office. The ambience was now closer to an accounting office. But I'd loved every day of it.

I regretted not having been closer to most of the people I was leaving behind, but in later years I was rarely involved in the social buzz and camaraderie of the office. It was partly the nature of my job the last thirty years, writing a daily column, winging it, a free agent or occasionally an untended cannon in the workplace. But it wasn't entirely that. Something in my own nature, not totally flattering, resisted joining the after-deadline bantering daily, although I happily butted in whenever some shaggy dog tale from the mining country was needed to save the conversation from becoming polished and genteel. None of this affected the respect and gratitude I felt for the people who on this December evening began to turn in their chairs to greet the departing figure with his desk mementoes and his rather grave demeanor. Somebody had been waiting for the light to go out in my office. As I began walking through the city room, the keyboarding stopped, replaced by applause. Some of them stood. I stopped and turned to the working journalists and waved an arm in appreciation. Some kind words were said by an editor. I didn't want to make a speech, and didn't. I spoke briefly and quietly, a thanksgiving. I said I would never forget them or the newspapering we did together.

And I haven't. But then I stopped, because I was about to break up, and that wasn't going to be very sightly.

I retired not being clear where life was going to take me but not especially worried about it. I wasn't sure about writing into the future. What I discovered first was what I was going to miss most. It wasn't the electricity of working against a deadline, although that was always part of the allure in the apprentice year I worked in Bismarck, North Dakota, the eight years with the Associated Press in Minneapolis, and the thirty-five years with the afternoon *Star* in Minneapolis and then the morning *Star Tribune*. To the mortification of the editors upstairs, in my years with the *Star*'s early morning deadlines I actually wrote a few final paragraphs in the composing room where the newspaper was being set in type before it was locked in for the big rotary printers. Bringing to the paper's thousands of readers the struggles of an obscure person, whose life had worth and the power to inspire, gave me a gratification and a sense of performing something of value that I don't think I could have found in another line of work.

What I found I missed most, though, from those days as a columnist, were the daily encounters with people who read the newspaper. They would call in the morning or at the most flabbergasting times, and I was reluctant to brush them off. But I enjoyed talking to the blowhards, the brooders, the self-constructed oracles, and the troubled. I especially liked the callers who had a cause, a grievance, a bureaucratic door to be opened or a story to tell.

Hundreds of those stories, in some form, made it into the newspaper over the years. The mossy axiom in the news business is that everyone has a story worth hearing. I discovered very quickly that this is by and large true if you allow the story-teller enough time to talk and yourself enough time to probe and be nosy. So for thirty years I often followed those small flares of serendipity that were touched by the ringing phone or by a letter. I've met some of the most extraordinary people in my life that way, and sometimes they became extraordinary people in the life of the newspaper reader. So I remember those hours more fondly than the big and public political brawls or the days at the stadium when thousands roared or got half-oiled in the parking lot. To be honest, I have to say there's a genuine wallop in telling that kind of story if you can stand loonies in the parking lot.

The stories and essays in this book reflect some of

the wanderlust that simmered after I left the city room to prowl exotic lands, seas, and the occasional mountain summit. They also reflect my re-enlistment now and then as a reporter and witness to the human condition on call by the *Christian Science Monitor*. It gave me some space to try to express the mood where I lived (from the heartland, they called it) during moments when the country bled, cheered, giggled or feared. There are pages in this book where I compare the then-and-now of an America I love as intensely as the most ardent warhawk, but wonder where it's headed with all of its power and late-arriving paranoia. There are other pages when I look into the heart and mind of an aging human being (me), ponder my mistakes and my amends, and wonder what constitutes true spirituality. I look at the playing field and marvel at the changes in what's there, in the galleries and on the television screens and try—although not very hard—to chalk it up to a different culture.

I look at the people who touched my life most deeply and enduringly.

The stories that follow are drawn from books I've written in my retirement, from the bumps and blunders of daily life, from my blogs (I thought I'd never say it) on the Internet and from my reminiscences. It was always a joy for me, with the newspaper, to settle one-to-one with the reader. If that happens here, today, I'm content.

—Jim Klobuchar
March, 2005

Walking Briskly Toward the Sunset

I. Days We Engrave

From Ginger Rogers, A Squeeze and a Promise

June 1997

Whenever I walk through a video rental shop, I slow down in the section usually labeled Old Favorites or Hollywood Classics. I'm rarely part of a stampede in that part of the shop. Cary Grant and Madeline Carrol don't draw salivating hordes in the twenty-first century.

I begin to take special care when I reach the "I" section. That's "I" as in *I'll Be Seeing You*. It was a movie. It was also a song. And it's never on the shelves.

The film *I'll Be Seeing You* came out during the 1940's, and I saw it, but that is not what the newspaperman in me remembers. I remember its star, Ginger Rogers, with a slight ache and a smile. When friends ask what celebrity I remember most vividly I usually skip through presidents, generals, kings, and quarterbacks and tell them about Ginger Rogers.

As I think back on my encounter with Ginger, my adolescent years and their world-as-theater mentality flood back, lifting me into a small reverie, and suddenly I'm sitting once again in a booth at the old Sheraton Ritz Hotel in Minneapolis, ready to sing a song, (which thank God I didn't) Ginger Rogers sits across from me at the chic little table and seems bemused.

In was early in the 1970s. She was in Minneapolis to appear in a style show for which the columnist Barbara Flanagan and I were co-hosts. A Hollywood star was usually

3

brought in to talk fashion and spruce up the show. Ginger was the featured guest that year. She was then in her late fifties and had recently concluded her sixth divorce. Over the years she had remained committed to physical fitness, and she was still chatty and lovely, still dancing and playing dramatic roles in

films. During our conversation backstage after the show she mentioned that she would be staying over in Minneapolis for two or three days to do some clothing promotions. She asked if it would be safe to jog through downtown Minneapolis, and if so, what were the best routes. I said it was safe and asked if she planned to jog alone. She did, but she preferred company. She smiled in a way that invited a gesture of chivalry. So here was a cue from Ginger Rogers, dancing partner of Fred Astaire, actress known to millions, including the audiences in the old Ely Theater on the Iron Range of northern Minnesota, where I grew up.

It didn't seem the time to be fumbling lines. I said I'd be delighted to be her partner.

I showed up at the registration desk of the Sheraton Ritz on Monday morning at the designated nine o'clock, wearing my running shorts and burgundy T-shirt. I asked the clerk to call Ms. Rogers, explaining that we had an appointment.

"Ms. Ginger Rogers?"

The same.

He phoned her room and seemed surprised when she emerged from the elevator a few minutes later in her running togs and her buttermilk hair. We ran up the Nicollet Mall, passing storefronts and weaving our way through clumps of pedestrians, some of whom gaped unabashedly at the sight of a celebrated movie star running through the streets of Minneapolis. We took a turn through Loring Park and then made our way back through the city to her hotel. The sun was out, and Ginger was relaxed and talkative and slightly exuberant. And then she asked, "Care to do a couple of steps?" I nearly froze. I dance like a sore-legged rhino. Here was Ginger Rogers asking me to dance in the middle of the sidewalk in Minneapolis. She extended her hands. "Be kind," I said. She was. She led and glided and did a turn, swung her arms and her hips effortlessly, bent her knee, and it was over. The crowd applauded. I offered a prayer of relief.

We had a light breakfast at the Sheraton Ritz before she went up to shower and change. She was thoughtful. She asked about my work, about Minnesota, and a little about my life. And then I had to tell her about the Ely Theater. "The movie of yours that I liked best…" I started to say.

She finished… "Was *I'll Be Seeing You.*"

How did she know?

"Fellows of your age remember it," she said.

I'm sure they do. It was certainly threaded into all the moony notions of romantic love that I'd developed during that impressionable stage of growing up. In fact, that film had somehow wrapped Ginger Rogers and a song into my life forever.

In the film she plays a woman convicted of a crime that sends her to the slammer, although it wouldn't get her two weeks of probation today. She's out on furlough when she meets Joseph Cotten. The story is sweet and wistful and weepy, and the lyrics of the title song draw a picture that no teenage romantic of the 1940s is likely to discard.

Ginger Rogers teased me. "I suppose you remember some of the words."

"I do. 'In that small café, the park across the way...'"

She broke in, half-singing, "The children's carousel, the chestnut tree..."

The wishing well.

When she left she thanked me for the run and for the company, lightly gripped my arm, half teasing again. When she died twenty years later, I dipped back into that little scene and remembered her words as she left the table, giving her jogging partner a droll wink.

She said, "I'll be seeing you."

An Innocent Puff of Smoke in the Sky, and Columbia Was Gone

February 2003

(Special to the *Christian Science Monitor*)

Even after the ominous first announcements, it seemed so innocent and clean flashing through the morning sky on our television screens, a streamer of white heralding one more arrival from space.

Maybe we've seen so many fictional encounters in space that we can't quickly absorb or accept the terrible spectacle of death in the heavens when it is soundless and comes to us masked as a swift and graceful plume of smoke splitting the blue sky above Texas.

Space is still a fantasy world for most of us. Its heroes are not warriors or gladiators confronting an enemy in arenas of violence. Space is full of wonder and mystery. It unites our imaginations with our longing to reach for and to find something beyond us.

The attention that today's television brings to a flight to the moon or to an orbiting safe house in space creates an audience that numbers in the billions. Yet it remains a personal odyssey for many who watch. The canvas of that journey is huge, the universe itself. Because it is, the event sweeps us for a few moments or a few hours into an experience that dissolves the boundaries of everyday life. It lets us soar and revel in a kind of psychic weightlessness in which we can frolic with the astronauts. It is exhilarating, and it seems harmless. It will all end happily on a runway in Florida or Texas, we tell ourselves. And the technology of spaceflight has advanced so far, and its success rate is so remarkable, that such an illusion about a space journey has become part of our experience as spectators.

But space travel is not harmless for the men and women who have become our escorts.

On Saturday morning, nearly 40 miles above the earth, the illusion broke once more, 17 years removed, almost to the day, from the awful fireball in the sky that ended the flight of the space shuttle Challenger.

The scientists, the engineers and the astronauts are constantly aware, of course, of the danger. And the viewing public is reminded of it at each step of the countdowns, despite the terse professionalism of those disembodied voices reciting the familiar litanies and dialogue between Mission Control and the shuttle commander.

Why, then, is the pain and devastation we feel so complete and stunning, so uniquely personal, when the spaceship falls to pieces before our eyes? We see grief and tragedy on our screens almost every day. We respond to it with anger or compassion or futility. On September 11, 2001, the death and destruction from an attack on the United States stirred Americans from sorrow to rage to retaliation and now toward war.

Tragedy in space is not like that. Although space exploration began as a harsh and expensive duel between the cold-war powers of fifty years ago, there is no special villainy in the stars today. It is a place for the exploring spirit to romp, and not incidentally, to do some required research, because it gets to be expensive floating around up there. It's the home of quirky contraptions like the space station and lunar modules, and we feel like kids again, watching the action. Schemes for the militarization of space are still on the table, but most of us look on spaceflight as almost pure adventure.

The star-wars are make-believe. The actual heroes of space are people who might comfortably be our neighbors, although they know all about the risk, and some of them are spurred by that risk. They are competent, brave and not gripped by illusions.

Slowly the face of the space crews has changed, so that when we looked once more Saturday morning at the stills of the team that rode spaceship Columbia, we were looking approvingly at a kind of family of man. Among the seven were men and women, people of color and a military veteran from Israel.

They seemed altogether normal and unaffected, no matter how professional. And perhaps that explains why, when the ghastliness of what we were watching became clear, our loss was so personal, why our mourning for their families went so deep.

What binds them most intimately to us? It is what seems to be that uninhibited sense of awe and delight that ignites both the trained astronaut and obscure trail hiker, when the path breaks clear of all the impediments and the sky is wide open and full of invitation and the view and the wonder of it seem to stretch forever.

George (Pinky) Nelson, a Minnesotan, rode the shuttle on three space missions and was one of the first astronauts to walk in space untethered to the mother ship. He is an astronomer and an educator and a trained airman. But he returned from one of the missions with the exuberance of an adolescent seeing the world for the first time. And so he had, the planet Earth in all of its distant marvels, from thousands of miles in the sky. Earth's precise features did not immediately reveal themselves. But there, stretching from the buff sands of the Middle East to the jungles of South Africa, was a great gash 4,000 miles in length that we call the Great African Rift.

It was a sight, he said. From lower, the astronauts could make out long lines of brush fires the villagers had started to speed up nature's fertility. They were somewhat startled. It was every day life on earth, our world, from space.

The distant skies are not the natural habitat of human beings. But finding out what is around a bend in the road, or beyond the hill, defines part of our humanity, and sometimes it is our dreams that unite the stroller with the explorer.

And so they did Saturday morning.

Editor's Note: Jim Klobuchar was one of 35 finalists for NASA's journalist-in-space project when it was canceled in 1986 because of the Challenger accident.

His Daughter Gives the Marching Orders—"You're In Charge of Lawn Signs"

November 1998

In the summer of 1998 my daughter, Amy Klobuchar, plunged into a take-no-prisoners political war for the office of county attorney of Hennepin County, which includes Minneapolis, its suburbs, and 800,000 lawns.

This figure is relevant because it indicates the approximate number of homeowners I was expected to canvass, looking for potential platforms for my daughter's campaign signs in the upcoming war for strategic grass. On the scale of battlefield enormity, my daughter compared it with the Siege of Leningrad. The idea on both sides was to smother the emerald turf of Hennepin County under a tidal wave of lawn signs so dazzling as to leave no doubt which candidate had greater momentum. This in turn would produce a soaring solidarity of voters marching regiment by regiment toward the ballot boxes. "The campaign could be won or lost on the lawns of Eden Prairie," my daughter solemnly revealed to the lawn-sign committee, and to its newly-installed field commander, me, on the eve of hostilities.

"Eden Prairie," I reminded my daughter, "is loaded with Republicans. If I show up in that town with your lawn signs and all those Democrat labels, they're going to turn loose the town dogcatcher. He'll probably come with a net. They're also going to serve me with an arrest warrant for illegal trespass."

My daughter shook her head impatiently. "They're Republicans," she said. "They're not sociopaths. We can get lawn signs there. The people of Eden Prairie will listen to calm reason, of which I know you're capable on your better days. Think about the big picture. We probably can't win a majority in Eden Prairie. We can control damage by making a strong showing." Taking note of my lack of exuberance over this assignment, my daughter turned off her phone and launched a full-court press to buck me up. She said I was super-qualified for the role of soliciting lawn signs in Hennepin County, from Rockford to Minnetrista. She said I was persuasive, borderline charming and, since I was now in retirement, mobile. She said she didn't know anybody in town who knew more about controlling damage than her father, who, she added with filial admiration, had made a whole career out of wading around in it at the Minneapolis newspaper.

"Be aggressive," she said. "The residents of Eden Prairie will love to see you."

In the days that followed, I saw no evidence of such devotion. I didn't reverse the Republican tide in Eden Prairie, although technically the race for county attorney is run without partisan labels. My daughter was endorsed by the Democratic-Farmer-Labor party of Hennepin County, her opponent by the Republicans. Both candidates spent campaign money ardently. It was a race my daughter ultimately won, nearly 24 hours after the polls closed, by the avalanche margin of 4,000 votes out of more than 440,000 cast.

I have no idea what part of that money was spent on lawn signs. I can tell you that by election day I had lost 10 pounds, experienced at least one verified charley-horse and one probable, and a blackened thumbnail where I'd swung my hammer at a sign stake and missed. I had been assaulted by three German Shepherds and one homicidal cat. I had 200 doors closed abruptly in my face and 250 if you counted screen doors. I was exposed to humility, euphoria, and sun stroke, usually in the same afternoon. I was also united with hundreds of people who'd read my columns and wanted either to greet me fondly as a daily visitor in their household or retaliate in some legal way for one of my opinion pieces that had left them enraged and blithering.

I'm not sure what to make of the incident in the big summer parade in Robbinsdale, where the gala crowd was packed eight-deep on the sidewalks and grass berms to watch an hour-long procession of fire engines, bicycling clowns, high school bands, bronzed beauty queens, and politicians. We were with the politicians—the fifth gaggle from the end. Flanked by her husband and their 4-year-old daughter, Amy worked the right side of the highway, shaking hands and exchanging high fives, while volunteers ran ahead distributing Amy literature. I walked the left side of the street wearing my "Hi, I'm Amy's Dad" t-shirt. The parade watchers were loose and amiable, for the most part, but halfway through the parade I noticed a woman staring at me from the curb. She seemed stricken, as though something alien and inexplicable had that moment entered her life. I walked over to where she was standing, smiled and said "Is there anything I can do for you, ma'am."

She gulped and said "Are you still alive?"

My first thought was to rescue the startled lady from this moment of stupefaction. I considering offering an apology. Then I realized she wasn't feeling awkward at all. Somebody told me later she was mad. No, she wasn't mad at me for making this unannounced return from oblivion. She was upset at a neighbor who'd been reading the obituary pages and found a story about some newspaperman who'd gone to his rewards, and the neighbor mixed up my name with the deceased's.

I'm not sure why I walked away feeling vaguely guilty for having unhinged a potential voter. But things tend to get nutty when your own flesh and blood is a candidate and people on the sidewalks are drinking beer and having a rollicking time yelling "Which ones are the clowns and which ones are the politicians?" My daughter handled all of that stuff with total aplomb and made friends out of the comedians. Once in a while she'd meet me in the middle of the street and we'd walk arm in arm for a few steps, though under her radiant smile she was giving me stage instructions.

"Dad," she said, "it's good to have you in the parade. Just remember that I'll do the politicking. Just try to stay out of arguments."

And I used to rock this person to sleep when she was three months old!

But as a matter of fact, I was enjoying being part of this moveable meat market of American politics. My daughter's campaign raised my capacity for bewilderment to levels I wouldn't have predicted. A couple of days after the Robbinsdale parade I walked up the driveway of a home on 57th and France in Edina—one of those idyllic suburbs where the daily celebration of success is threaded into every flower bed and three-car garage. Thrusting myself into these graceful jaws of Republicanism, I rang the doorbell. A middle-aged woman came to the door and said "Yes?" I introduced myself. She beamed her approval. "Oh," she said, "I loved the columns your father used to write."

I thanked her but had to reflect privately that within a couple of days I'd been given up for dead by one woman and consigned to a nursing home by another. The thing you have to remember as a lawn sign solicitor is to forge ahead no matter how chaotic the mixture of illusion and reality.

The toughest crust of reality that I ran into came from a guy living on Normandale Road in the manor district of West

Bloomington. He had a round, ruddy face and thick neck, and he was muscling a big boat around the front yard getting ready for Up North or the races on Lake Minnetonka. I walked across the lawn and introduced Amy's candidacy.

"Aren't you the guy who used to write in the newspaper?" The same, I said. He looked me up and down with uncompromising disdain, not unlike a hanging judge regarding a four-time offender.

"Liberal, right?"

"Sometimes," I said.

"Democrat, right?"

"I once voted for a Republican for municipal judge," I said.

"When?"

"In 1958"

"You wrote in favor of tougher gun control laws, right?

"I did."

"How often, would you say?"

"Anytime I could."

"Well, I don't have any time for people who call themselves Democrats. So what are you doing here? What do you want? Money? What?"

"Well, sir," I said, "I just came to your lovely home and yard on the chance that you would think well enough of my daughter's candidacy to allow us to put a lawn sign on your beautiful lawn."

He didn't bother with musings or deliberations. He said, "Is that all you want? Be my guest. Put it wherever you want."

It was up in two minutes, possible record time in West Bloomington.

Tell me about politics when you have a few dozen hours.

A Walk to an Ethereal Mountain

October 2003

At three in the morning in the Himalayan village of Landruk a powerful amber light flooded the inside of my tent and bolted me awake. I sat up in the sleeping bag, dumfounded, and zipped open the flap of the tent's vestibule to investigate the source of this high altitude light show. I found myself gawking at an enormous full moon that had climbed above the summits and ignited the Himalayan landscape.

It lit the snowfields of Annapurna South and seemed to liquify the exposed granite of the cliffs that rose above the glaciers of the Annapurna massif stretching for miles to the north. I had stood in the midst of these mightiest of mountains before, yet the scene burned itself indelibly into my brain. And somewhere above that chaos of ice and stone rose the fluted peaks of Machapuchare, where we'd camped a few days before.

You'll have to forgive a certain amount of mush-headed romanticism when I get around to Machapuchare. I have an oil of it hanging in the stairwell of our home. It's the most elegant mountain I have ever seen. The Hindus call Machapuchare sacred, and if I were a Hindu I'd light some sprigs of juniper beneath it to show my reverence. I'm not a Hindu, but I've considered lighting the juniper. The mountain is that lovely, isolated, and introspective. Its peaks rise into the sub-stratosphere like the tailfins of a great fish.

I began climbing and trekking in the Himalaya of Nepal 25 years ago. In those years we pronounced it Mahtch-ah-pu-char'-ee. with the emphasis on the next to last syllable. Technically, some of us learned later, it's pronounced with the emphasis on the syllable before that. It's too late for me to change. The earlier pronunciation gives it a lyric cadence that it deserves.

We trekked for 11 days in the heart of the Annapurna Range, five of us laboring through a collage of sensations from dazzlement to exhaustion. We traveled through a vast rollercoaster of flagstone staircases and forests of sycamore and rhododendron. Gauzy blankets of moss repelled the sun's strenuous attempts to intrude in those musky woods. The monkeys had better luck. They chirped and quarreled and mocked the plodding trekkers while hawks and eagles wheeled slowly a couple of thousand feet above us. It went that way, day after day, and it might just as well have been a dream. Bob Distad, Gertrude Juncker, Kazia Gajl-Peczalska and her son from Warsaw, Kazimier Peczalski, were my companions. From the fairy tale setting of the Pokhara Valley in Nepal, we trekked with our Sherpas and porters into the Annapurna Sanctuary, whose centerpiece is a vast amphiteather that puts the Himalayan traveler almost within touch of these gigantic fortresses of rock and ice. The scale of the mountain architecture is enormous, yet we felt an uncanny intimacy.

Still, Nepal is not a place where the reality of the world's turmoil magically disappears in the midst of its high world of ice and sky and the mumbled mantras of our Sherpa companions.

On the second day we reached Gorapani, the historic Horse-Watering Pass where caravans of ponies carrying salt from the Tibetan plateau and the old Silk Road meet the rice caravans from central Nepal. The Nepalese government, locked in a civil war with rebellious Maoists, had pulled practically all of its army, police and civil agencies out of the Annapurna district to avoid incidents in which trekkers or tourists might be caught in a firefight.

Despite seven years of fighting, tourism remains Nepal's biggest source of foreign revenue. The Maoist movement grew out of the desperate poverty in which most of the Nepal's 25 million people live. While the Maoist attacks and bombings try to avoid what western military people would call collateral damage, they have generated a war that has resulted in thousands of deaths among government personnel and Maoist fighters and periodically shut down some of the Nepalese meager infrastructure.

In the Annapurna district, most of the militancy takes the form of a shakedown of foreign trekkers and tourists. The extortion is widespread. "Give us a thousand rupees apiece (about $13) as a donation," the usual pitch goes. "We need it to fight the government's corruption."

We were met in Gorapani by a young Maoist political officer, who invited me into a kitchen tent where our Sherpas were preparing supper. "Namaste," he said, in this case, "good evening." I said Namaste. The Maoist delivered a brief speech denouncing the Nepalese government, which was then receiving military assistance from the United States and probably India. The Maoist said he had no animosity toward the American people, although this avowal of friendship didn't necessarily seem entrenched. He wasn't showing a weapon but he probably carried one and he had friends outside the tent. He said he meant us no harm but would admire a thousand rupee donation apiece. The company that provides us with our Sherpas, porters and equipment had counseled us to comply with the Maoist shakedown. It turned out not to be necessary. Our lead Sherpa volunteered 5,000 rupees from the company to cover its clients. The Maoist wrote a receipt for the extorted cash and left the tent with the folded rupees in hand.

Despite this predictable scene, the Annapurna district presents no shortage of trekkers. We met hundreds of them, from India, Germany, Australia, Italy, France and Japan.

We saw few Americans. But the Nepalese government maintained stricter control of the country's other major trekking area, the Solo Khumbu of Everest, Ama Dablam, Thangboche. Except for another Maoist orator we met on the trail, we were otherwise unmolested. And by the time we reached the Annapurna Sanctury and the Annapurna base camp, the Maoists had faded into the forest. We hiked the two miles and 2,000 vertical feet from the onetime Machupuchare base camp to the Annapurna base camp, set in a marvelous cirque of glaciers, moraines and white world.

Ahead of us an avalanche glissaded down the ice chutes of Annapurna South, falling more than 2,000 feet before dissolving into a cloud of powder that rolled a half mile across the amphitheater floor but posed no hazard to the gaping travelers. In front of us stood the enormous bulk of Annapurna I, the first 8,000 meter peak climbed more than 50 years ago by the French. In a Hindu chorten, a kind of offering site near the lodges that now serve trekkers at the Annapurna base camp, was a memorial honoring Anatoli Boukreev. Anatoli was the powerful Russian mountaineer who may have been slandered by some accounts of the Everest disaster in the late 1990s. He was killed in an avalanche on Annapurna I during an attempted winter ascent a year later. I'd met him on the trail to Dingboche a few days before the Everest disaster.

But this was a day for the sun and for living things in the Annapurna Sanctuary. The sun poured out its nurture and healing on the Annapurnas, the legendary dwelling place of the goddess of the harvest. Waterfalls flashed off the hanging glaciers of Annapurna I and goats scrabbled in the meadows.

This is a huge world, the Himalayas. It can be a savage one, as it has been for Tibetan refugees seeking freedom in their barefooted journey over 20,000 foot mountain passes. And yet to the seeker it can be endlessly alluring and, on days like this one, absolutely benign. And also divine?

The Goddess of the Harvest, Annapurna? Why not?

A Beloved Clown Hears His Last Laugh

July 29, 2004

(Special to the *Christian Science Monitor*)

What was he worth, Bob Hope? A million laughs for certain. But for his American public, there was so much more that never registered on the applause meters.

It didn't matter the venue. It may have been a radio studio in Los Angeles or a dusty airstrip in the South Pacific, or on the back of what he called a Morocco-bound camel in one of his slaphappy films with Bing Crosby. Or a dilapidated hospital room, where he sat comforting a dying child.

For the better part of a century, Bob Hope made the world better because he made it lighter and funnier. In the midst of the greatest war in history, he stirred America to smile and howl. For its fighting men and women, he relieved for at least an hour the terrible hazards and the fears of tomorrow.

Before he died at the age of 100, he must have known, should have known, that very few Americans reached the levels of popularity and trust that Bob Hope earned over a lifetime.

Trust? The GIs for whom he gave thousands of shows and hundreds of thousands of volunteer hours can tell you about trust, and today many of them will have to clear their eyes remembering. Half a world away from home, the sight of Bob Hope on the stage, with the crackle of those rapid-fire gags and that celebrated ski-slide nose gave those GIs an unmistakable bridge to their country and the sound of home.

It didn't much matter that Hope was born in England. Not many people in show business caught the American idiom and the heart of its humor—whether hilarious or droll—with his nimble sureness. The ad-lib outburst and his one-liners, flitting off the top of his pompadour pate, wowed his audiences and his comedic victims alike with their zany thrusts. "I was well on my way to being a juvenile delinquent," he told an audience, recalling his adolescence. "When I was sixteen, I had more hubcaps than General Motors."

And: "Those were really tough times. I wouldn't have had anything to eat if it wasn't for the audience throwing stuff at me."

"Our neighborhood was tough. We had the typical gang. You know, Shorty, Fatso, Skinny, Stinky. Then there were the boys."

He needled his show biz rivals mercilessly and, of course, they loved it. Toward the end he reflected on his travels. "In my lifetime I saw the Berlin Wall come and I saw it go. George Burns [another nearly indestructible comedian who died earlier] can say the same thing about the Ice Age."

Bob Hope may have worn better than the Ice Age. He was the mugging face of NBC for more than five decades. On the edge of 90, he told the *Monitor* how he escaped the potential oblivion of vaudeville and the nightclubs. "I was going nowhere," he said, "until I decided to try something new. The leading columnist in those days was Walter Winchell, and he had a rapid-fire style. I decided to hit the audience with one gag after another and not wait for them to laugh. Just keeping firing one-liners. It used up lots of jokes. My first movie was a little two-reel masterpiece called 'Going Spanish,' which was shot on Long Island. When Winchell asked me if it was any good, I replied. 'It's so bad, when the cops catch [public enemy] Dillinger, they're going to make him sit through it twice.'"

But in the midst of the Depression, Paramount gave him a role in *The Big Broadcast of 1938*, hardly remembered today as a rival to *Gone With The Wind*, which was filmed about the same time. But out of that movie emerged a tune, "Thanks for the Memory," which became his theme and his signature.

American filmgoers knew him best for his wacky partnership with Crosby in the "Road" series, in which insiders insist the actual script for their off-the-cuff dialogue lay in shreds before the pictures ever reached American screens. He haggled with Bing from North Africa to Singapore, and when he wasn't doing that he was rolling his eyes at Dorothy Lamour in her swaying sarong. Hope and Crosby golfed together for years, raising millions of dollars for an endless stream of funds and causes. But it is the American service men and women away from home who will treasure Hope's legacy most intimately. It didn't have to be a crisis. He entertained in Korea, Italy, Vietnam and in the desert, on the deck of a carrier or in a barracks in the South Seas. If Americans were lonely, Hope enlisted. He once did a special show for a company of Marines, and the commanding officer told him that they were going into battle the next day.

Hope learned a few days later that 60 per cent of the company had been killed in that battle. The next day he had to be funny again. It was a load. He carried it, a soldier in his own way. He was on the road, in the air, and at sea virtually every Christmas. He logged millions of miles. He remembers the tenderness of some of those visits.

He married Dolores Reade in Erie, PA in 1934, and his wife came with him on one of his earlier tours. She sang 'White Christmas,' and the soldiers loved it.

How do you define credibility after a lifetime like that? He met and told jokes about the nine presidents. None of them ever told him to knock it off.

"How can you get angry at an American treasure?" a White House press officer said.

He was that, and a treasure still.

A Woman Writes Her Name
For the First Time, and Cries

June 2003

A Hindu woman of Nepal in her 50s, humbly dressed and hesitant, turned to a friend with a question. On her forehead was a painted red dot, a tika, common to her tradition. She was asking for a writing pen. The lines of her brown face deepened with what seemed to be the solemnity of the moment.

In the back country of Nepal, one of the poorest countries on earth, she was one of 30 village women in their shawls and long dresses gathered to conduct an open-air business meeting.

Until that day, she had never written her name on a document. Until a few weeks before, she had never written a word, didn't know how to read or write.

She will never be rich. Life will be a daily struggle for her, perhaps to the end. But on this day, her world changed, and she wept for the wonder of it.

Sitting at a battered pine table, skewed slightly out of plumb on the dirt floor that constituted their business center, were the group's chairperson and loan officer. On the table in front of the small semi-circle of the seated women were small stacks of rupee notes, most of them faded and crinkled but still the going cash of the realm. The women were there doing the business of a bank—their bank. They were taking applications for loans—theirs. They were also making weekly payments on their outstanding loans. The average payment, including interest, amounted to $3.00 weekly. The average size of those loans amounted to $70.

The chairperson looked through two pages of notes that recorded the group's current transactions and the payments.

There were no defaults on outstanding loans. Everybody with a loan was current.

The women were serious players in a global movement—for some a life-or-death movement—of which only a microscopic part of the western industrialized world is aware. They were building tiny enterprises—selling grain in the market, making clothes to sell, fattening goats, weaving baskets—to lift their families and themselves out of poverty and out of oblivion.

It's variously called micro-credit, micro-enterprise or microfinance, and it's been working now for more than 30 years. Today nearly 100 million "barefoot capitalists," which means some 250 million people, counting spouses and children, are living better lives as a result of the loans they receive by this means. For some it has meant the difference between life and starvation, between school and lifelong ignorance for their children, between health and HIV-AIDS.

The woman with the wrinkled face had been taking loans for five years, using the money to buy material for the children's clothes she sold out of her house. She was applying for another on this day. The micro-credit system, funded in part by donations by foundations, the World Bank, governments and individuals, operates under rules of due diligence. The borrowers have to sign their applications. Like millions of others around the world, she had been pressing her thumb on an inkpad and signing the application with her fingerprint, the only acceptable method for people who can't write.

On this day, the woman stood at the table and asked for a pen. Because her micro-credit group was receiving courses on family planning, disease prevention and other social development, she had been taking literacy classes.

Slowly and laboriously, she scrawled her name on the application.

She straightened up and stared at what she had written. For the first time in public, she had written her name. She put her hands to her face and began to cry. She had an identity. She had written her name on the paper, like all of the others who could read and write.

Her friends gathered around the trembling woman, hugged her and cried with her.

It was the liberation of one person from the humiliating straightjacket of illiteracy, and it had come to her as the reward for a risk. She had taken the risk, executed her first tentative stroke of independence, on the day she joined the solidarity group of borrowers, pledging to pay back a $40 loan with interest, in four months. She used the money she received as a lever to make enough clothes to make a profit of $15, with which, in turn, she was able to buy more and better food for her family.

That scene raises a provocative question.

How much *do we really* know about the economics, how much do we know about the humanity—or lack of it—in what we deftly call the war on poverty.

Waste and corruption, the theft of billions of dollars of donated development money? We know about that. But are there some lower-level schemes that actually work? Most of the agents of our information, the highly-scrutinized "media," aren't in the business of trying to deceive, yet they have not been especially robust about giving visibility to the performance of micro-credit. But about poverty, we're often headline readers. Do we know or remember that in America itself there are 34 million people living in poverty?

Stereotype thinking afflicts all of us. The agents of our information aren't spared this condition. They congregate each day in the conference rooms of hundreds of American newspapers and televisions channels. They come with computer printouts and bullet digests of what's happened around the world in the last twelve hours or the last ten minutes. This is a news huddle and these are the editors and directors. The subject: what are the stories today, local, national and global. What are today's calamities, threats of war, triumphs and scandals. What goes on the front page or at the head of the newscast? The news gurus go down the list—the Middle East, business, crime, government, politics.

Somebody mentions Africa. "What's new in Africa?"

"The same," a voice says. "AIDS. Corruption. Civil War. Starving Kids."

That was the answer for more than a decade. It got old and repugnant. Masses of TV watchers and newspaper readers tuned it out. These were people whose lives had no more room for stories of far-off AIDS or far-off tribal war. They tuned out news from Africa with a yawn or a sigh of boredom. It expressed their futility. They were asking a question: How or why would you try to rescue those places? How can you understand them?

It was a predictable response after all of those years of slaughter and starvation, overthrows, generic corruption and the disappearance of some of our foreign aid, meager as that has been at times. Goaded by Britain's Tony Blair and other European leaders, the world today is beginning to take seriously the poverty, hunger and profound malaise of Africa. It is committing more money to meet the catastrophe of AIDS and starvation as a means of curbing tribal warfare and stabilizing the continent. It will take decades. There isn't much more shock left in the tragic story of Africa and for a long time we didn't want to hear any more of it. But because we didn't, we might have missed—and are still missing—the beginning of another Africa. To this Africa you can add parts of Latin America, India, Indonesia, Bangladesh, the Philippines, eastern Europe and elsewhere.

Tens of millions of people in places such as those, often the scenes of tragedy and human despair, are finding a way to lift themselves out of poverty. They don't ride on the magic carpet of mythology. Their vehicle is the humble small loan—as little as $50—and the password to their new lives is "micro-credit."

Many of these people, and their numbers run into the

millions, were once all but abandoned. But today they are building new lives and often doing it with a buoyancy and camaraderie that can startle a visitor whose mind is programmed with images of a land helpless in the grip of epidemic and anarchy.

Small loans in themselves are no fresh discovery. What's dramatically different is the concept of a structured and disciplined micro-credit made possible at the outset by donor money from foundations, individuals, world bodies, and a range of nonprofit, government, and financial institutions in the industrialized countries. The goal is to make micro-credit groups self-sufficient. Many already are. Those more than 100 million enterprisers have evolved in little more than 30 years, and the best news is that it is happening today at an even faster rate than before.

As a movement of human liberation, micro-credit (a.k.a. micro-enterprise or micro-finance) comes with a public relations handicap. As a label for a dramatic transformation of lives, the term micro-credit doesn't fill the air with electricity. But what it means is that people around the world who were once denied the most basic access to banking and financial services now have the ability to borrow on credit. The tiny businesses that are being developed as a result range from making woven baskets in Bolivia to fattening cows on the Maasai Steppes in Africa to operating a flower stall in the middle of Manila. There are hundreds of other mini-enterprises that produce significant income for millions of families.

The network of non-profit organizations and government agencies that make the loans insist on repayment and strict accounting. Amazingly, they are proving to be the best loan risks on earth.

It's vital to remember that the huge majority of the smaller entrepreneurs live below or near the poverty level. Micro-credit works because the borrowers in most of the plans do their banking—applying for their loans, setting aside savings, paying the interest—as part of a group of their peers, anywhere from 30 to 50. The group has authority to approve loan applications, and through its elected board it keeps tabs on the repayments. It works with loan officers who birddog every transaction and know the strengths and troubles of each borrower.

Essentially it's a family council whose members are related not by genes but by a common resolve to dig themselves and their families out of poverty.

The individuals involved don't have the collateral required to get a loan from a commercial bank. But with micro-credit, the group becomes the collateral, guaranteeing repayment of the individual loan. If Borrower X gets sick or falls behind, the group will know about it and respond accordingly. Over the years these unsophisticated borrowers, many of them illiterate, and with an average income of only one or two dollars a day, have repaid their loans at an astonishing rate of more than 95 per cent. Their performance is astonishing because commercial banks can't match that repayment rate on the loans they make.

Those loans have been repaid faithfully because nearly 90 per cent of the borrowers are women, whose first and last commitment is to *their children*. And that's where the bulk of the income from micro-credit goes. The stories of these families are creating a new frontier of life in Africa and elsewhere. It dramatizes what is possible when the human will and ingenuity are joined by the good will and partnership of new friends thousands of miles away, people who understand the drive for dignity and education that fuels the ancient tradition of the entrepreneur.

Susan Wilkes, my wife, and I have been exploring this social phenomenon together for some time now, from different but complimentary perspectives. I have been leading mountain climbing, trekking and camera safari expeditions in Africa and the Himalayas for 20 years. Susan's work in developing countries and international outreach has taken her to Bhutan, the Middle East, and Africa. The goals we share in our social commitments came together in the belief that the poor in the developing countries have the same right to dream as we do, and that the same ambitions and yearnings that drive our lives stir in theirs.

What's different is the opportunity. In our travels, Susan and I visited some of the small enterprisers who were making use of micro-credit in South America and Egypt, Nepal, Bangladesh and sub-Saharan Africa. The cultures were different, the colors, tongues and faces. The gratification we read in the eyes of those people was the same in every country, every village. They had found a way, modest but exhilarating, to express those ambitions, to shred the fears of poverty and to turn the light of hope on their years ahead. Some day, many of them vowed, their children would go to college—in LaPaz, in Kampala, in Nairobi.

We saw some of those children, on their way to college diplomas.

As a result of those travels we wrote a book, *The Miracles of Barefoot Capitalism*, to widen the awareness of the program and its potential among people of good will who might be drawn to its power to change lives. Our purpose in our explorations in Africa, South America and elsewhere was to take a realistic look at micro-credit, at what its advocates believe is *one of the most reliable roads* yet to alleviate world poverty and to empower the voiceless, especially women. Americans raised in the codes of self-reliance and the supremacy of free and private enterprise instinctively applaud the concept of micro-credit in the poorer countries—when they learn about it. Apart from major financial institutions and nonprofit organizations, scores of American family foundations and individuals looking for deserving causes have made that discovery in recent years.

They will make one more discovery. The surest way to bring a people out of poverty, to curb sickness and to stabilize a nation politically is to educate its women. With education comes empowerment. With women's empowerment the children have a chance.

It's a goal worth the millions of lives it would save and enrich.

II. Up Close and Personal

A Cry From a Lonely Room

August 1998

I felt a condemnation that gave me no escape. It left me dazed and shaken. As I crossed the hall to my room in a small chemical-dependency treatment center in the Minnesota countryside, several men and women, fellow clients, passed me in the hallway. We usually nodded in passing, but on this day I didn't see their faces, didn't hear their voices.

The condemnation was my own. It was as though I'd been forced to watch a film of the last thirty years of my life, secretly made, that revealed, frame by frame, a person I'd never seen, and a path of destruction I couldn't have imagined. The cost in emotional injury to those closest to me, the cost in broken relationships and violated trust, kept piling up with each frame, until the shame was so painful that I wanted to scream at myself in the mirror: "How could you have done this?

But I avoided the mirror, and it wasn't a movie I saw. It was a blackboard that chronicled the wreckage of a part of my life, and the wreckage that I'd inflicted on the lives of others over the years in a rampage of self-gratification. It had been my bag, my pace, my thrills; me first, a chase, renewable daily. I had piled my energies and ingenuities into it, ignoring the cost. I'd refused to make the moral assessments. I refused because the other side of my life was filled with excitement and strokes from what I saw as achievement and the perpetual motion it fostered.

But on this day I was confronted for the first time with the full weight of the injury that my alcoholic lifestyle had caused. When I got back to my room, I closed the door to escape into aloneness. But privacy gave me no relief. No amount of self-accusation did, nor the recognition of a make-believe faith, nor the taking on of guilt. The numbness in my body couldn't erase the shame. Finally, I knelt, helpless to do any more.

'God help me," I said.

I expected no answer.

But one came.

It was a beginning.

Until my last breath I will not forget that moment in May, 1993, in a small chemical dependency center in the town of Cambridge, Minnesota. I relive it often, whenever I need replenishment, whenever the first shadows of doubt appear, or the first threats of alienation from someone or something important in my life. And each time I experience those dull but worrisome murmurs of a reversion to my self-absorption and evasions of the past, I close my eyes and shout a warning to myself:

"Don't go down the road again."

It is a red flag whose meaning can't be mistaken. It says, "Don't appease your vanities. Don't weasel around the truth. When your temper makes you pig-headed, admit your arrogance. When you're lost, call for help. When you're tempted to do it your way and to hell with a better way, remember where that conceit took you in the years before you recognized the folly and the stupidity of it."

It took me into divorce court. It took me into a stonewalling relationship with my younger daughter, Meagan, that lasted fifteen years. She overcame discord in her early years to become a *summa cum laude* college graduate in her thirties on her way to a fulfilling life. Those conflicts in our earlier relationship have been resolved, thank God, and we are at peace with each other.

My trauma in the treatment center ripped away all of the self-constructed buffers and escape hatches I'd created to insulate myself from the truth about my multiple lives. The life that I thrust in front of the world, in front of my closest friends, was the one I admired and cultivated. That life was not an illusion. I was a newspaper columnist, read by thousands and I'd guess respected by many of them. I did television and radio, wrote books, spoke to church conventions and jock strap smokers. I communicated almost non-stop. By longevity if nothing else I could exert some influence on community issues when they needed an airing or a prod. I was an entertainer, a public conscience, a town crier. Somebody called me a minstrel. I was a teller of stories and a singer of songs.

The picture seemed reasonably accurate. I shared the lives of people who would otherwise have been obscure or voiceless, but whose lives had something good and even inspiring to say about facing adversity, pain or death. The best of those stories sometimes gave the reader a chance to lift his or her own life out of obscurity. If it was a love story, it might have been the reader's own. It didn't need glamour or big names. It didn't need spectacle or controversy. I didn't write it to showcase my sensitivity. The beauty of commitment, of unbreakable love, is something universally recognizable. The truth and simplicity of it are indivisible. And the days when I wrote that kind of story are the ones I later treasured most. They redeemed the combativeness or the burlesque or the heavy-handed wisdom of some of the other columns. The love story was the worthiest and most believable story I could bring into the reader's day and, for a few minutes at least, it forged a connection between the storyteller and the reader that was real and intimate and touched by trust.

I remembered writing a story of a 84-year-old man who walked two miles to a nursing home each day to visit the woman with whom he had lived for 34 years. His love for her hadn't diminished through the years of their eroding powers to enjoy life and each other. Each day he would put on a fresh shirt, a tie and a suit or blazer and bring a flower to her where she sat in the lounge. For him each day of their partnership had been an occasion, and his daily visits became small anniversaries.

It didn't seem to matter to him that her decline was much faster than his, although their ages were close. He still read and walked in the parks. He had breakfast with friends near the apartment house where he lived, and went to movies or a ball game with them. He had worked as a salesman and long ago retired, but the relaxed kind of courtliness with which he treated customers, and the woman of his life, were still part of his carriage and his personality.

Erect and slender, he'd walk into the nursing home with a broad smile and his flower. It was his daily appointment with the queen, the attitude he carried into the nursing home every day, and it wasn't fanciful or an act. He felt it, and it showed. She never seemed overwhelmingly receptive. From the beginning she grumped her way around the nursing home, made few friends and trusted none. Her once attractive face had tightened into a permanent scowl that told the rest of the residents she preferred the isolation that was sped by her deepening surliness. For all they cared she was welcome to it. When his hand touched her wrist she often ignored it. Their conversation on most days would begin with predictable "how-are-you"s and end in silence. When he thought he was annoying her with his gestures of affection, he would sit quietly for awhile and then get up to leave, touching his cheek to her forehead and smiling.

In her last year, she stopped recognizing him on most days. She didn't respond to his name. A nurse would repeat it. "Who?" she would say, and fall asleep. There was no further conversation between them. So he just sat with her and held her hand, and gave her the flower. Their meetings went that way for months. And on the day she died, he brought a bouquet of flowers to the nursing home staff in her name, and wrote a note to them in a hand that was beginning to tremble. "Thank you for all you gave us," it said. "She was a beautiful lady, and I loved her."

On days when I would write such a story, I sometimes stopped in the middle of it because my glasses were fogging and I had to struggle not to weep openly over my keyboard. Each time that happened, a question emerged from those soggy introspections and I needed to ask. "Why can't I have that kind of love?"

I couldn't answer then. It was only after my recovery from alcoholism was underway that I began to see the truth of my self-deceptions in my marriages and my relationships. I thought I was giving love, but it was a stilted, contorted kind of love, at my convenience, a self-serving love that met my obligations to my wife and children (but only occasionally) and gave me all the approval that I thought I needed—my own.

Is this a hard judgment in retrospect? It is. Can't it be softened by the hindsight reminding us that when two human beings live together, drift in ultimate disillusion and then split, the fault can't rest on one alone? Well, yes, that's a consolation and possibly an escape. The human condition, nobody's perfect, all that.

But the breakup of both my earlier marriages came down to me: my selfishness, my timetables, my satisfactions, my world.

I've said this in my sobriety to both of the women to whom I was married. They said "Let's get on with our lives." I've made that apology to my children, my stepchildren, to the others whose affections or trust I abused. They said you still matter to us, and some of them said, "I still love you."

The peace I now experience in the aftermath of those traumas is comforting, but not quite complete. There were years of their lives that were irreparably damaged by my self-indulgence or my neglect.

I feel that remorse at times today, and grieve it when I do. It's not an anvil I haul around because I remember that the yesterday of my life, whatever its pain, is gone. And the life I have today is still endowed with reasonable energy, curiosity, rewarding work, and the fulfillment of a love I couldn't have foreseen, and would never have been worthy of, before the world changed for me. The gift I've received from those who forgave me, and my reconciliation with God and with those closest to me, have made these the best years of my life.

And today I know I'm capable of love and can give it truthfully. That is a grace. I can wake each morning and tell myself, "You are loved, you are forgiven, you have something to give." And that thought gives me peace.

Remembering a Good Man
and the Lives He Saved

January 2005

When I learned he was gone, I turned out the light and cried like a child. It was too late in the night to make calls—better simply to remember the grace and reconciliation he brought into hundreds of lives, including mine.

We met 11 years ago when he congratulated me on my first milepost as a recovering alcoholic: one month of uninterrupted sobriety. I remember feeling surprise and a twinge of awkwardness. In the long and uneven history of reluctant abstinence, 30 days without a drink didn't seem to qualify me for the Olympics. I wasn't totally sure that he was serious. Maybe this was some harmless initiation rite impressing the neophyte with the long grind ahead down a road that had chewed up millions of vows and shaky resolutions.

It wasn't an act. He was serious. He was a big guy with a quiet and unhurried voice and a face that seemed to invite trust. He had the modest presence of a man who long ago had ridden out a storm and come to terms with a kinder self. He smiled often and without provocation. I don't know if this made him the stereotypical lawyer, but he *was* a lawyer, it turned out, and a good one. We sat in a coffee shop that day, and my education at the age of 64 began to expand.

He said 30 days was an achievement. Tomorrow, he said, it would be 31, and 32 the next. He didn't tell me to do the math, but the idea was hard to mistake. If I didn't get absorbed with the road ahead, he said, it would be simpler. If I didn't let myself be smothered by guilt looking back at my follies and self-indulgence, it would be easier. It would be easier if I dealt honestly with the offenses of my years of alcoholism, made my apologies and asked those I'd wronged to forgive me. I needed to know that I didn't have to walk that road alone. And in the end I would be free, released from the temptation to wear a mask or to reach for false and fickle suns of gratification. I would find that the make-believe world of lubricated good times could never be as good as a new and sober today, because today we could look at the world with clear minds and a new respect for truth. And if we weren't totally rid of the self-deceptions and shams of our drinking years, at least today we could now recognize our personality warps for what they are and try to blunt some of the jagged edges.

He said "we." He was then in his nineteenth year of sobriety. He'd been a cop and then a trial lawyer. His name was Gerald Freeman. There were times in his drinking career when he'd given a reasonable impersonation of a hell-raiser, but that was then. What he became in the next thirty years was a man whose wisdom and internal strength rescued the lives of scores of men and women in his profession, and scores of troubled people who had never known him until alcohol shredded their lives. He listened to those who were willing to put the pieces back together and to restore value to their lives, and he became their advocate.

Alcoholics Anonymous wisely counsels anonymity among its members, although because of its work in raising public awareness, alcoholism does not carry the same degrading stigma it once did. The rule of anonymity is not set in granite. The identity of some members, because of unusual circumstances, is difficult or impossible to keep secret. In this, Jerry and I were alike. I wrote of my drunk driving case and subsequent treatment when I was a newspaper columnist in Minneapolis; Jerry was a founder of an organization to restore alcoholic lawyers to sobriety. We became friends and, a few years ago, he became my sponsor in AA. At first we lunched often, talked about our lives, about the Vikings, occasionally about politics—although we weren't always working with the same alphabet there—and later we talked about his declining health. He was careful not to brood about it. But he had trouble with his legs, and then more serious organic trouble that began taking him away from his work, and from the AA meetings, where he was always a figure of great esteem.

After each luncheon, we'd clasp hands and pray together and then exchange a hug. Our lives moved on different tracks and we were never drop-in friends. But we didn't have to be that. Ours was the friendship of understanding, respecting what we saw and felt and heard in the hours we were together.

Our meetings weren't all that solemn. Jerry had the storyteller's gift, robust and creative and all but inexhaustible.

His health eroded. He had respiratory break-downs, sieges of pneu-monia. Later his disorders compounded and forced him into extended hospital treatment. He underwent operations and rehabilita-tion. He never showed a symptom of giving up. Three and four times he appeared to be at the edge of death but rallied. His disposition seemed never to change. Incredibly, he was still courteous and interested when he had the energy, lying on a hospital bed, scarcely able to breathe.

I began to remember the instinctive decency of his conversation. Once I told him of a grief that kept recurring, something out of years past. It was fostered by a regret so painful that I kept digging it up, wanting in hindsight to redress something that was beyond reach. We were silent for a few moments. I looked up and found my friend trying to smile, but doing it rather damply. "That was yesterday," he said. "A lot of yesterdays. This is today. You're all right. You can let it go."

I visited him at a hospital in Rochester in late December a few days before my wife and I left on a trip to Europe. By then he was in and out of consciousness, sometimes recognizing his visitor, sometimes not. He had stopped breathing once, but his wife's swift call to hospital attendants brought him back. He was asleep and briefly alone on the day I visited. I stood at his side, feeling helpless, saddened beyond words, confused. Then I called his name and told him I was Jim, coming to see him. He began to open his eyes and tried to speak. Nothing came. His eyes closed. "Jerry, I brought a Christmas card." There was no response. I didn't want to leave because I knew I wouldn't see him again. I'll never know whether he heard me. But I wanted to give testimony to this lawyer friend of mine, with whom I had prayed, who had said today is what mattered, so give it your energy, your generosity and your care. I spoke as clearly as I could and told Jerry Freeman what he had brought into my life.

I told him my work had been filled with the faces of people we call famous. Some were admirable people, some not. Among all these, I had never met a man who moved me more profoundly than Jerry Freeman. This was a man of integrity and commitment but still a regular guy in any crowd, yet always in search. I remembered the trip we shared in the Holy land. We'd seen the historic sites of Christian, Jewish and Islamic faith, the church that had risen above Golgotha, and we'd affirmed our baptism in the waters of the Jordan. And then we had stood together and looked across the deep gorge that is now called the Wadi Qelt, and saw the Roman road, carved out in the dirt of the far slope, virtually unchanged in 2,000 years. It was the road that Jesus Christ walked from Jericho to Jerusalem.

No one spoke. The sight reached across the chasm of centuries, overwhelming and indelible.

Before I left the hospital, I touched his arm and his cheek and thanked him for all he had given me. I don't know if he heard. The night I returned home from our trip I looked at my email letters and learned that Jerry had died on Christmas night. His loved ones were with him and he died in peace. He couldn't have known the number of lives he saved or changed. I can only tell you that mine was one of them.

Romance on an AARP Card

...he way through the movie, *The Insider*, ...n the role of a health expert, is agonizing ...o tell CBS' *60 Minutes* all he knows about ...scheme to drive millions of smokers into ...ng a touch of agony, too, as I placed a ...he armrest separating my seat from the one occupied by a woman I'd invited to see the film.

My intention was to find some serviceable way to take her hand without (a) shredding her concentration or (b) damaging her rotator cuff. Mentally, I squirmed. I worried about the protocol of hand-holding in the movie at my age and at hers, which was manageably less than mine. I worried about the reception my harmless sortie would receive. But I also worried about the possibility that she might simply mistake my movements for Golden Age fatigue.

I'm trying to tell you that this was a date, and it wasn't easy. After two marriages, intermittent bachelorhood, re-established friendship with the two women I'd married; after two major surgeries and a quiet withdrawal from all hotbeds of amour; after six years of relative calm and order in my life, I met a woman named Susan. It was because of her that, in the fourth year of my retirement, with two versions of the AARP card wedged in my wallet next to my Social Security number and Medicare card, I was once again exploring the dicey thickets of romance.

I'm now getting conditioned to life on a trapeze.

I don't hold Susan responsible for that. After the marriages and my recovery from alcoholism, the passage into adulthood of my children and the arrival of a granddaughter, I'd pretty much decided that my life was now more or less in equilibrium. With daily journalism behind me, I was free to write books here and there, and to escort the clients of my travel club to the Himalaya and East Africa. I could still climb mountains, find the time to appreciate the odd play or film, have dinner with friends, and reflect with gratitude on a life now predictable and mostly tranquil.

With the arrival of Susan Cornell Wilkes in my life, that picture—of a genteel withdrawal from the volatilities and confusions that most psychologists now call "relationships"— was a picture pretty much shot to hell.

I started sending her e-mail letters, ignoring the outside possibility that in the pace of her professional work—giving away money for family foundations, a.k.a philanthropy—she might not have time to read them, let alone reply.

But she replied. My letters often ran to 600 or 700 words. Her answers were economical but generous, e.g., "What a wonderful letter. I read the first two pages. Were there more? Maybe I'll see you in three weeks after I get back from New York."

I'm not sure this announcement constituted grounds for a love lasting through time. But we both sort of hung around. She was attractive and well-spoken and defied all attempts at type-casting. She was tender and bright, zany in spurts, oblivious of time and absolutely committed to uplifting the voiceless of the world. We'd met at a couple of gatherings we attended with friends and associates. She sometimes wore a black skirt and royal blue blouse that seemed to send wisps of cool flame rippling through her blonde curls. She wore silver around her neck and wrist, and she was just very hard to ignore in any room. Because I occasionally mentioned Nepal and the Inca Trail in some of my conversations, she assumed I was a travel agent. Which is why I was puzzled when, at our first breakfast together, she started talking about frequent flier miles. I had only a moderate interest in this line of discussion and discovered that she'd lived for seven or eight years in San

Francisco. She was enchanted by the city in all of its variegated skins and tongues, and for a hundred other reasons, though she didn't seem to be all that crazy about Minnesota as a permanent home.

"We lead the world in producing taconite tailings," I said loyally.

She smiled at this rustic show of Iron Range pride and admitted that the San Francisco crowd was largely ignorant of such things. This goaded me into a surge of cross-cultural outreach. I gave her a signed copy of one of my books and confessed that I'd been in daily journalism for forty years, most of it in Minneapolis. Since she'd been in Minneapolis for only two years, she said, she had not yet subscribed to the Minneapolis newspaper and had to stumble through the world's daily events with her *New York Times*. Saying this, she smiled luminously in a way that suggested she was capable of reform. This in turn stirred me with the fugitive hope that she might some day entertain the idea of ice fishing on Lake Minnetonka.

Her life history, she said, was quickly told. She had grown up in the east, lived in Washington D.C. in her formative years, got her college education at Harvard, and in her early professional life helped launched the Up With People program that propelled its high-energy youth all over the planet with their song and dance. She was the mother of three adult children, divorced, and now immersed in philanthropy and non-profits management.

I asked about her interests. She said she loved to read, cook and explore. She said she was excited by places like New York, San Francisco, Africa, South America, Central America, India, Kathmandu, the Middle East, Bhutan, Spain, and Little Rock, Arkansas, where she had lived for years during the mid-life of her career.

This didn't leave much. I was tempted to ask about Spitzbergen and Azerbajzan, but my companion was now in full stride of revelation. There was no bravado or self-assertion in any of this. What it was, she said, was a celebration of her freedom of action and thought. She'd spent hundreds of hours prowling museums and sculpture gardens. She loved ballet, theater and painting, from Van Gogh to goofball posters at the sidewalk exhibits. She could spend days in the Smithsonian and often did. She read the works of Socrates, Plato, James Thurber, Jack Kerouac and P.D. James. She was neutral about curtains and drapes because she needed light and big windows wherever she lived. I tried to avoid staring numbly. It's an attitude that does not work aesthetically with gaping jaws. But I did have to breathe. I'd suppressed that act throughout her remarkable recital. I had no idea of her taste in music. I decided to risk. "Do you go to symphony concerts?"

"Yes, whenever I can."

And opera?

`Whenever I can."

So now we were well and truly launched. We talked Chopin and Brahms, Mozart, Beethoven and Rachmaninoff for almost an hour. The waitress was starting to look hostile. We gathered our coats. I asked whether she went to the movies. "I do. Doesn't everybody?" I brought up *The Insider*. She'd heard of it. "Would you like to go, say tomorrow?" I asked. She said, "Why not?" I took this response for something less than unchained exuberance. She probably saw that and added, "I'd love it."

She may have. I didn't invest a whole lot of heart and gusto in our post-mortems at dinner after the show. If you want to know the truth, I was brooding. It went back to the scene of my takeover of the armrest. She couldn't possibly mistake my intentions because I held this posture without flinching for 20 minutes. Finally our hands came together and the moment was warm and heady and touched with some really advanced stuff, such as the exploration of wrists and knuckles. After 10 minutes of it, though, she abruptly withdrew her hand, leaving me with an empty palm and a deflated psyche.

I apologized at about the time the pepper shaker arrived

at our table. "What for?" she asked. "I had a grand time." I brought up the handholding. I said I'd been presumptuous and a damned fool.

"Nothing of the kind," she said. "I liked what you did. But the way we were positioned, I had my arm caught between the seat and the armrest and I was afraid of getting my elbow torn off at the roots."

She said she'd like to go to more movies. Her explanation lit up the night. When I got home I phoned her apartment and thanked her for the evening. She said she meant it about more movies.

"When?" I asked helpfully.

"As soon as the swelling in my elbow goes down."

She wanted to know if everybody in Minnesota held hands like lumberjacks.

The next day I turned in my chainsaw to the Salvation Army.

Romance and AARP Card (contd)

Iron Range vs. San Francisco, an Uphill Fight

April 2000

From our e-mail file, January 5, 2000, 10:44 a.m.

Dear Susan –

I've reviewed my conduct at your dinner gathering last night and made some evaluations.

Not wanting to appear *gauche* at table when you offered another serving of your chicken and rice, I said "Thank you, no." Evaluation of this decision: It was a mistake. Your chicken and rice could have hauled down $38.50 on the menu of any restaurant in town.

When you offered a second helping of the salad, I said "Thank you, no," which since leaving the Iron Range I've been taught is proper conduct in Kenwood. Evaluation of this decision: It was a mistake. Your romaine salad would have routed all challengers at the Minnesota State Fair.

Hanging around to talk, after your friends left, on the transparent excuse of helping in the kitchen. Evaluation of this decision: It was not a mistake, except for the time when I stepped on your toes trying to unload the dishwasher. I enjoyed your friends, the dinner, you, and the walk to my car in the snow afterward.

Do they teach all of these things in Arkansas?

—Jim

You may already have come to the conclusion that one of my problems in discovering more about this woman was the woeful obsolescence of the rules of engagement with which I conducted my courtship. For example, I really wasn't sure how she would react to a simple hug when I arrived. I mean, to hug a woman you've met only two times would have been something terribly *déclassé* when I was younger. But today we hug the cashier at the carryout counter at Lunds Supermarket. We hug the accountant who does our taxes. Never in the history of humanity's pawing and groping have so many been hugged so irrelevantly. A couple of years ago my doorbell rang a minute or two after a small colony of my relatives had left in a welter of the usual grapplings and squeezings. It was snowing hard and I mistook the man at the door for one of my relatives. I hugged him routinely, thinking I'd forgotten somebody. It turned out to be the UPS delivery man. Not wanting to seem ungrateful, he hugged me in return.

But here was Susan Cornell Wilkes, a party-giver of some renown in San Francisco, where she lived for nine years before being coerced to Minnesota by an attractive corporate offer. This eventually led her into the field of foundation management in Minnesota and back into international development, her primary passion. Before San Francisco she'd lived in Arkansas for eighteen years, where her acquaintances as part of her non-profit and international outreach projects for the state included Bill and Hilary Clinton. Before that she'd lived in Washington D.C. as a member of a family that practically arrived with the Mayflower. Somewhere in all of that she'd co-founded the Up With People youth program, had three children, divorced, and—it seemed to me—looked perfectly capable of dealing with the world without a bear hug at her doorway by one of the indigenous Minnesota snowmen who happened to have known her for a few weeks. Further, this was a woman who was no stranger to the shifting relationships of a mobile past, so much so that her father could exclaim, with a mixture of amazement and resignation: "Life with Susan is one long series of dramatic announcements."

And why not? Her family tree included the late, great actress, Katharine Cornell, and her later life was speckled with a variety of rebellions from an adolescence during which she'd felt boxed in by the demands of puritanical religious dogma.

But no dramatic announcement accompanied my arrival at the doorway as the first of the invited guests. What did greet me was a beautiful woman, transformed from our the night at the movie. Her smile raised enough genteel heat to launch a summer breeze through the frosty foyer. With lightning speed I hustled through my options of behavior. I could shake her hand. But if you did that, you would also run your way through the Louvre. I could airily brush her cheek, which nobody in Minnesota has done since statehood. I could kiss her lightly, which would have been presumptuous.

So naturally I gave her a hug. I can't actually tell you I was timid about this. She wore a turquoise shirt wrapped in a bow at the waist and a pair of black slacks and silver earrings below her cropped blonde hair. I have to tell the truth. I didn't really give a damn whether the other guests arrived or not.

But they did arrive, and we formed a rather sedate company in the living room before a psychologist and I hooked into polite but clenched-teeth argument over the American intervention in the Balkans. Our hostess floated genially over these proceedings, fed us all, lavished us afterward with coffee, and—the psychologist and I having made peace and established mutual esteem—Susan Cornell Wilkes received unanimous congratulations for the production.

When she saw me to my car I kissed her goodnight. "You were a star," I said. "You managed and entertained and cooked and served and somehow you made yourself almost invisible doing that."

She thought that was gallant of me to say.

And why did this quietly begin to matter to me?

I was seventy-one at the time, and the idea of a romance had pretty much disappeared from my arsenal of likely possibilities. It wasn't age by itself. It wasn't a matter of feeling old, or even of *being* old by today's liberal standards of defining age. But it was an age that had to deal with some sexual limitations resulting from surgery performed by doctors in the simple interest of keeping me alive. It was a choice I was given in the face of a prostate cancer that looked very lethal under the microscope. The choice came to this: surgery with the risk of damaging a rather important nerve, or who knows what?

In the years after this and other surgeries, I felt strong and alert. My energy bins seemed well stocked. I climbed and rode and skied and wrote and filled most of the day with something productive and, I thought, fulfilling enough to myself, and often to others. But being able to please a woman adequately, and seriously, was something else to ponder. And I did ponder it, no matter the durable maxims about "There's a lot more than that to a successful relationship." That there is. And I thought, "Hey, how many other guys go through emotional obstacle courses like that, my age or younger?"

The answer, of course, must be in the millions. Susan and I subsequently discussed what we would or could bring into a relationship. I brought up the limitations part of it. I said the usual gyrations and bliss that are part of a relationship would be available to us but it would take a little preparation, and then it could be normal. I explained it at a time well before the promotion of bedroom additives on television had become epidemic, crowding out beer and SUVs. She thanked me for my candor, waved off any anxiety about it, and it was quickly a non-issue.

But this was still early in the dance, and we had just begun to explore. In reflecting on my own life, I'd already begun to ask myself what shape these "later" years were going to take, to ponder how to go to the edge without doing it ridiculously. What part do I give to family, meaning my two daughters and granddaughter, and to service, a.k.a volunteerism and church? To what degree can I continue to sustain the kind of work—writing, organizing travel—that stimulates me? And what about leisure? It's not exactly a disease.

There'd been one, major and transcending change in my life seven years before, and it made these decisions manageable. I'd undergone treatment for alcoholism. Sobriety cleared my head, made me accountable for the times in my life when I was arrogant and self-serving and abusive by neglect. It put truth back into my life, and it had reawakened me spiritually.

Riding home from Susan's party, I thought for the first time in seven years that there might be a person in my life to whom I could extend the kind of love of which I'd seemed incapable before sobriety.

But what did I really know about her, this appealing woman of breadth and achievement, approaching 60, with a history of past relationships as cluttered as mine? And what made me think she might be as curious about the possibilities as I was?

Two days later I invited her to a concert in St. Paul, where Beethoven's *First Symphony* and *First Piano Concerto* were featured. On the e-mail I signed myself "The Pest," because it was the third e-mail in two days.

She answered:

"I'm dying to go. Do you mean tomorrow? If so, yes, please let's do it. And knock off this pest stuff. I like being with you—in fact I'm starting to miss you when I don't see or talk to you."

It wasn't exactly one of Elizabeth Barrett's sonnets. But it read just as well.

Romance (contd): He Prepares Dinner

Nervous Host Enlists Mozart

January 2000

I approached Susan Wilkes' arrival for her first dinner at my place with a candid assessment of my limits as a host.

My advanced skills in entertaining house guests are limited to a swift response to the doorbell. After that I silently throw myself on the mercy of their manners. Ideally, my guests are babblers who change conversational course without an inhaled breath of air. To cover my thin virtues as a party host, I expect my guests to be social hummingbirds, full of wisdom and transfixed by my oils of Lake Superior raging in a storm off Anna Mae Peterson's Cliff and Surf Motel north of Two Harbors. This allows me to be a genial impresario, scoring points by patiently waiting for a pause in the verbal torrents to take the drink orders.

But that's one more recurring crisis I face trying to mount an image of the courtly host attending to all esoteric tastes in a time when most of today's refrigerators groan under the weight of a half ton of flavored soda water. I don't drink any more, which means I don't keep crates of French wine around the house. I do maintain one bottle of Burgundy and one of French white so as not to be typed as hopelessly barbarian by my more discriminating friends. What I usually offer, if you have to know the truth, is a choice of Diet Coke, Hoh! Mendota Sparkling super pure spring water, the wine, and decaffeinated coffee. If there's a request for tea I have go into the tank because my last packets of Darjeeling tea from Kathmandu ran out two years ago and I haven't thought to replace them. If none of the above prove irresistible I do have an escape hatch—Florida's Natural Apple Juice, Pasteurized, Not From Concentrate.

And now here was the doorbell declaring the arrival of my dinner guest, Susan Cornell Wilkes, whose corporate dinner engagements the past few years had included some of the swishiest hotel restaurants in San Francisco, New York, Washington and Little Rock, Arkansas. But right there was an entry point for a little *savoir faire* of my own. I thought about Little Rock. It bucked me up for the program ahead. I concluded that anybody who'd spent eighteen years in Little Rock, as she had acknowledged, can't be totally drenched with sophistication. I opened the door and she made a relaxed and homey entrance, awash in a blouse sporting muted tones of blue and off-white, but wearing black slacks that suggested she was ready for whatever lay ahead, Sunday football or Debussy. In fact, I had programmed both, with an explanation.

I worked hard not to be obvious about my small acts of readiness. I know you'll agree that trying to orchestrate the scene under these conditions is terribly bourgeois. So I didn't fill the stereo with Mozart and Chopin. I did open with Mozart's *Clarinet Concerto*, and from there moved to some piano intermezzos from Brahms, to Rachmaninoff's *Rhapsody on a Theme by Paganini*, to Bruch's *Violin Concerto*, then to Debussy's *Prelude to the Afternoon of the Faun*.

Clearly, I did not arrange the program to impress Susan Cornell Wilkes. The music was universally romantic and needed only the right volume control to contribute pleasantly to the ambience while remaining unobtrusive. I'll admit that I experimented with the volume control before she arrived and settled on a sound level where the music could be heard comfortably in the living room without destroying normal conversation. I'll also admit putting the Mozart concerto on hold until the doorbell rang. I think you'll agree this was permissible hostmanship. A convenience. It would make my guest's entrance simultaneous with the beginning of the *adagio* movement, which I knew to be music that turned her eyes to dew.

"Oh," she exclaimed after I took her coat. "That's marvelous music. It's one of my favorites. Did you know that?"

"Yes," I said. "I've had it on pause for ten minutes. If we'd been in the concert hall the orchestra would have mutinied." Some of my three-year-old birch logs were crackling in the fireplace. "And I love the smell of the fire," she said. "Can we watch it for a while?"

I replied that it certainly was an option, adding that at the moment the Vikings were in the middle of a touchdown drive in the late-season. If it didn't strike her as being too suburban, would she mind if we watched a few minutes of television? I was working on a book about pro football and what was happening at the moment might be relevant.

"I'd love to," she said. "I don't know football well so you'll have to tell me what's happening." I put Mozart back on hold and we watched Jeff George taking the Vikings downfield.

I didn't have to tell her what was happening.

"It's third and eight," I said. "If they don't make eight yards and a first down, they'll have to..."

"They'll have to punt, won't they?" she said.

"Right. They will unless they decide to try a field goal."

She had a question.

"Aren't they too far away for a field goal?"

They were.

I said it was all right if she took off her shoes and put her feet on the couch.

She smiled, took off her shoes and put her feet on my knees.

It was awhile before I liberated Mozart from his quarantine. I made some random asides about the action and she thought they made sense. "You know this game very well," she said. "Have you written other books about it?" I said I had, but sometimes I had more fun teaching a football clinic for women. This news abruptly lit her curiosities. She wanted details. I said I taught seven sessions each fall for years, explaining the differences between red dogs and hot dogs, trying to demystify the game and to bring the women into the huddle to learn all about the gobbledygook that forms the language of football, all about the hut 1, hut 2s and hut 3s.

"We had an annual field trip to Chicago for the Vikings-Bears game at Soldier Field," I said. "My students all came wearing those Brunhilde braids and horns and purple helmets, and the Bears' fans would try to spill beer on them. I told my people to turn all available cheeks. This was well-intended advice that a few of them misunderstood and as result provoked more cascades of beer and the customary insults. I had to crack down a few years later, though, when I got a call in my hotel room. On the trip down I'd distributed complimentary Viking swords, little rubberized toys about three feet long. The phone call I got Saturday night was from the police."

My guest was now trying to suppress laughing jags. "What did the police call about?"

"They wanted to know if I had any connection with this group of wild Minnesota Viking fans, all of them women. I was wary. I said 'Why do you want to know?'

"They said four of these people were in one of the bars on Rush Street threatening the customers with those crazy swords, and there would be hell to pay unless somebody got them out of there.

"'Officer,' I said calmly, 'escort them out of there but don't confiscate the rubber swords. They'll need them in self-defense at the stadium tomorrow.'"

My warriors arrived at the hotel at three a.m. with their swords, which I, of course, confiscated on the spot.

Susan Cornell Wilkes thought this recital was so bizarre and great that it deserved a thirteen-week TV series.

By the time we got to the roasted chicken in front of the fireplace, the birches were long gone and needed replenishment from my dwindling supply of soggy oak. The evening, though, was cozy and somewhat evocative for both of us, because by common consent we'd both offered extended monologues to bring the other up to date with our lives and to uncover some of our histories.

I first have to explain the chicken. I don't cook. Since the end of my second marriage I'd subsisted in my modest town house on a variety of salads, TV dinners, produce from the stores and odd medleys of fat-free fare from the delis. The roasted chicken came from Byerly's hot food showcases. I told the attendant, my favorite food handler in the store, that this should be a special roast and would she steer me away from some nondescript turkey.

"These are chickens not turkeys," she said.

I nodded a silent apology and fled home fifteen minutes before my guest arrived.

Susan talked rather thoughtfully and candidly for two hours. I told her of the relationships in my past, of the spasms of promiscuity in it. I told of my re-discovery of truth in my recovery from alcohol, some of the ugliness of my earlier life, and the relative calm in my life today. I said I had some wonderful female friends, but none of them partners of mine.

She told of earlier relationships, her divorce, difficulties in the lives of her grown children that had resulted in part from her career commitments. She told of the stability that had come into her life as a result of an independence she had not felt before. She said she was able to live alone without a reckless search for a male companion, but she'd welcome a committed, monogamous relationship with a man.

The nominations did not seem to be closed.

She said she valued sex but wasn't ready to go to war if it wasn't guaranteed every night.

I thought this sounded reasonable. We talked some more, laughed a little about the length of our testimonials but made no pledges and lit no more fires for the evening.

She called when she returned to her apartment after the drive home.

"Thanks for having me over," she said. "It was a night to remember."

Note: Romanticists among the readers will be delighted to know that a year later the two were married. Like most of their peers they have struggled occasionally but remain in that happy condition, attending concerts together, traveling in Africa and Nepal, mourning the national political trends together at breakfast and now and then playing four-handed arrangements of Beethoven, not well but ardently.

III. The Odd Elixirs
of Up North

The Instant Allure of Pine Needles

September 2004

If you turn the globe to North America and locate northeastern Minnesota, you'll will make a discovery that I admit won't shake the cornerstones of world geography.

Northeastern Minnesota is roughly equidistant from the North Atlantic, the North Pacific, Hudson Bay and the Gulf of Mexico. Pause to do the calculations. It means that for a thousand miles, in every direction, northeastern Minnesota is completely separated from all seawater, barking seals, ocean breezes and Bermuda triangles.

You could call that serious isolation. For a boy growing up in northeastern Minnesota as I did, being marooned so far from the established trade routes and legends of the deep might have produced disruptive personality kinks and actual neurosis. Intuitively I looked for compensations. I found them on the day my father and I got into the family car and drove from my home town of Ely in the mining country down the hair-raising swerves and drop-offs of Highway 1 to the shores of Lake Superior.

I was six at the time, and my first glimpse of those immense waters was electrifying. They spread to the horizon, filled with a million sequins dancing in the morning sun. Lake Superior is not formally described as an ocean, but that is a mere technicality. For me it was an ocean. I grew up surrounded by lakes but this was a sight for Balboa. I could see the water whirling off the rock cliffs below us where the surf sent its impatient combers vaulting high above the beach, and I implored my father to hurry down the woodsy headland to the shore so I could touch the lake and feel the spray.

In those years it wasn't easy to get to Lake Superior from the Iron Range. Highway 1 was built and paved in the tracks  of an old logging road, before technology arrived in the northern Minnesota woods. Most of its right-angle turns and seemingly bottomless dips were never straightened out or seriously reformed by the pavers. Highway 1 was one of the last of the navigable roads in America for which the motorists' standard preparation included Dramamine tablets and empty stomachs before departure. But we did finally arrive on what was and is called the North Shore Drive, and I touched the waters of Silver Bay and heard the roar of the surf, and Lake Superior became my ocean.

I have returned to it scores of times since, driven its shore, boated in it, flown over it, bicycled around it, skied beside it and once actually swam in it.

My wife and I have explored the North Shore of Lake Superior several times since we met. Each time, while we're riding along the waters and peering out into the bays, I sense that she is rather heroically trying to purge her brain of the nearly ten years she lived in San Francisco.

When this happens I drift into the role of Lake Superior's biographer.

"This is a huge and amazing body of water." I tell her near Castle Danger. "It's a sea. It actually has a six-inch tide. That is documented and it's undeniable."

"You don't say," she says.

"I do."

"I know. It's the sixth time you've said it in the last three years."

I'm about to argue that this is rank revisionism and unworthy of a cultured woman, but she's probably right. Moreover, she bats her lashes waggishly as she speaks, in what is clearly intended to be a gesture of tolerance braided with affection.

That mood—affection—is the one I feel more than any other when I revisit this watery vastness. It is too cold for sunbathing, for surfing, for swimming, for dawdling, almost too cold for fishing or for boating and certainly for erotic grappling under the stars. But every life has scenes and places and textures that identify our passages and our rites in how we have come to live and what we have come to treasure. Those sensations recur without the dimming of time or infirmity. For me, the woods and waters of northern Minnesota never fade among those scenes and markers, and the sights of Lake Superior, austere as it might be but still with the power to arouse wonder and humility, are a part of that. The pine forests and waterways and the stunning grace and marvel of the aurora borealis in the northern sky in midwinter—all of these lifted me into my adulthood and into the wider world. Not far from here was a lake where we canoed as boys. We imagined ourselves as the reincarnated Magellans and the islands ahead of us were the islands of Cape Horn. The waves were a little smaller, which was good, because nobody wore life jackets in those years.

Sifting through those images in our ripening years and returning to those lands and waters does not have to be an exercise in soupy nostalgia—although there's no special reason to knock soupy nostalgia, either. They are places of restoration and thanksgiving. A few miles beyond the town of Two Harbors we rode past a little clump of cottages and motel units. There was a sign: "Closed." It was Anna Mae Peterson's Cliff and Surf Motel, where I'd stayed a dozen times to hear the surf thrashing and thundering before piling into the bedroom. Anna Mae was the aging princess of the North Shore for hundreds of guests over the years. Her guest rooms were immaculate. The sea was at hand. The little lounge with its doughnuts and popcorn was open and available all night for insomniacs or dreamers, but mostly for people who wanted to sit by the hour with a hot chocolate in hand or a book, treasuring an interlude of unity with wild nature.

Anna Mae battled the reality of expenses and maintenance and mounting years, and finally had to relinquish what, after the death of her husband, she loved most in life.

I tried the door to her nearby home. It was locked by the real estate company. I looked into the sitting room where we'd talked so many times. The furniture was gone. The house was empty.

Without words I thanked Anna Mae for all she and her northern sea had brought into my life.

We rode up the Gunflint Trail fifty miles to the lakeside cabin owned by a friend in Minneapolis who had invited us to spend the weekend and had given us the key. We stopped at Johnson's little supermarket in Grand Marais and nearly bought out the store. "It's a weekend," I reminded my wife. "It's not an expedition to Baffin Island." She said we needed enough to fend off starvation in case we were snowbound. I said it was August. She said in Minnesota it's sometimes hard to tell the difference between August and January. I raised a white flag.

We built a fire and read into the night. We looked out on the lake and felt embraced by the quiet and the starlight. A few waves lapped timorously against the dock and boulders. The next day was glorious, and we canoed Seagull Lake, sloshing around in the breeze, cooked a steak for dinner, lit a fire, read while the flames cracked and Schuman's *Piano Concerto in A Minor* played on the family's 78 rpm records. And finally on Sunday we hiked for two hours on the Kekakabic Trail.

I thought I'd never set foot there again. It was something you did years ago if you knew the northwoods and had energy. The Kekakabic Trail was built 70 years ago by the kids of the CCC, the Civilian Conservation Corps created by FDR to give thousands of young men some work in the worst years of the Depression. It was built as a fire trail but was never intended for serious hiking. I remember hiking the 45 miles with two friends 35 years ago, through the woods and bush, around a dozen lakes, from the Gunflint Trail to the Fernberg Road near Ely. And I remembered trying to ski it a few years later, following the plastic blazes hammered by the Forest Service into the trunks of the Norways above the snowdrifts. For a newspaper series I called it the "Trail of the Blue Diamonds," which is what the blazes resembled. It was a good try, but a nightmarish experience. The government weather station officially recorded 40 degrees below zero on the first two nights, and our sleeping bags degenerated into the consistency of cast iron. We called it off after four days. The slush just below the snow pack on the frozen lakes built up snow chunks eight inches deep on the bottoms of our skis. We had to clean them every 30 minutes in brutal cold.

But in the last week of August in 2004, this was the Kekakabic Trail once more. There wasn't another soul on it. We walked in from the road, through the aspen and pine and trailside patches of wild blueberries and raspberries. The odd jay or seagull flew overhead and far below us in the marsh, three ducks made a V in the water. There wasn't a sound. I looked for blue diamonds on the Norways, eight feet off the ground.

There were none. This was another time, a slower walk, an older woods, and a visitor quietly restored.

A Cyclist Finds Heaven
on a Misty Road

July 2003

There are days that the bicyclist remembers for years—every eruption of sunflowers, every distant barking dog, and each bend of the road. The sounds and scenes blend into a quiet yet dazzling mosaic of a day at peace in the country, and the memory never seems to dim.

There was such a day in the forests of Wisconsin. On this day the sun is rising in the northern woodlands, sparring briefly to dispose of the mist that slips and tiptoes its way through the hardwoods and pines and hazelnut bushes. The sun has hours to burn, and will make short work of the mist, a diehard straggler of the northern night, but in the early morning their encounter turns the countryside into a phantasmal scene of shifting gray shapes and pale amber streamers of sun bent by the retreating fog.

Motorists may grumble when they find themselves enveloped in such atmospherics—it's dangerous, and it costs them time—but bicyclists want it to last forever. Around a curve in the road in the three-quarter light a deer appears, motionless at the edge of the highway. The bicyclists stop. The fawn is staring at them, but with no disposition to run. If they'd look overhead they might have seen a seagull doing slow acrobatics above a stand of Norway pines. And suddenly the world, for those few moments, comes to a stop. Here you have to allow the bicyclists a moment of proprietorship. If you don't ride a bicycle in the early morning in the north woods, you can't quite experience a discovery like that.

Well, all right, forever sometimes has a short shelf life. But for the hundred-odd riders on our twenty-ninth annual Jaunt With Jim tour, it lasted at least through the 12 miles from Drummond to Mason, a town which bravely asserts its current population as something around 122, although not so many decades ago it was home to thousands, to sawmills and rumbling freight trains carrying millions of board feet of white pine to the lumber yards of America. In fact, standing near the town's dormant tavern, beyond a clump of trees, is the manor of a long-since-departed lumber tycoon. It was built by Cass Gilbert who, almost nobody in Mason will hesitate to tell you, also designed the U.S. Supreme Court Building, New York's Woolworth Tower, and the State Capitol of Minnesota.

It's something you learn on a bike ride. Today Mason falls into a civic category somewhere between "ghost town" and "the sticks." But these are hard and dismissive words which a town like Mason doesn't deserve. It's something else you learn on a bike ride. Most people who still live in Mason don't work in Mason. The industrial town of Ashland on Lake Superior is twenty miles up the road and the resort towns of Cable and Hayward support sizeable payrolls to the south. What people who still live in Mason do on a Sunday morning in June is to lay out pounds of caramel rolls and rice crispy bars in the village fire hall and spend an hour telling the captive visitors what a totally amazing place Mason was.

How many towns of 122 can you name that maintain a museum where you can see black and white photos of log stacks four stories high and a switchboard with plugs and sockets where a hundred years ago people called in and asked for "central." The switchboard operator at "central" knew every shred of gossip in town, of course, and usually went to her grave with tight lips and the satisfaction of having saved half the marriages in town and a jail term for the city council. Today we can call Bangkok by cell phone. In those days they used party lines, and no secrets lasted very long because those were the glory years of eavesdropping.

We hated to leave Mason. Although I have developed a slow-burn of indignation for the clear-cutting frenzies of the timber empires of a hundred years ago, the details and lessons of that slash-and-burn era, when they're encountered in the congeniality of a bike ride, tend to be more absorbing than inflammatory. This, after all, is the history of the extractive industries.

A cross-country bike ride is no place for polemics. The other suspects of group conversation—weather, football, sex, weather, football, the stock market and weather—are usually overwhelmed by the traumas and random bliss that color the memories of the bike ride itself. Most bike riders are merciless historians. This is a highly competitive, savage field of scholarship. There are people on this ride who actually went on the Internet to produce the approximate number of Army worms that infested our campground in Hibbing, Minnesota two years ago. Somebody is going to say there was no rainstorm like the one from Cannon Falls to Chaska in 2003, during which one of our riders actually entered a outfitter shop in New Prague to consider buying a pair of fishing waders as a condition of finishing a ride. "Wrong," somebody will say. "The rain was so bad under the statue of Big Herman in New Ulm that it put six inches of water in Donna Ranallo's tent, and she got into a plastic garbage bag to stave off hypothermia, and the tent flap opened and she floated out into the campground."

This is truth. And on down the road, somebody might say of the 2003 ride in Wisconsin: "It was uncanny. Every day sunshine and practically every day a breeze at our backs. It was that way from Spooner to Drummond and then in Bayfield and on Madeline Island and Park Falls and Ladysmith..."

You have to give cyclists a little slack. We did have two hours of rain from Ashland to Hurley. But you had to forget the rain when you remembered the entrepreneurs at the Hurricane Hut in Bayfield on the shores of Lake Superior. The proprietors claimed they had gone on an inventory trip at the Mardi Gras in New Orleans and came back with an arsenal of garish beads and painted glass necklaces which must have retailed for 10 cents apiece. Word got around. Bicyclists thronged the Hurricane Hut to buy ice cream and the glass beads that went with it as a premium. I'm talking unisex beads. In time the huskiest, beefiest, slickest male bicyclists all ran around wearing beads and glass, and I want to tell you I needed great ingenuity to explain all of this to the cops in Hurley.

Alone Among the Wolves

March 2005

There is a place in northern Minnesota where you can imagine yourself at the end of the earth. You can't do it in summer. In summer, northern Minnesota gives you blue water galore and blabbering forests, streamers of sun kissing the reflections of birches in the rivers, and loons wailing their mysterious language.

But in the middle of winter you can find a place that must remember the Ice Age. You can go for days and experience the eerie sensation of being the last man on earth.

In a book called *Over Minnesota* I described a place "just 200 miles from the glassed citadels of technology and metropolitan life, where the traveler can stand by starlight on a frozen lake and listen to the soul of the wilderness. It comes in a concert of voices, the baying and howling of wolves. The sound seizes the traveler's brain and transfixes it. The howling wolves evoke another time in our relationship with nature, an unwritten time without calendar, dominion or boundary."

This is the Minnesota northwoods in winter. Like most people drawn to the spectacle of unfenced nature, I'm excited by the stratospheric beauty of the Himalayans, by Africa and Yosemite. But I was born in Minnesota's north country. The waterfalls and stands of blue spruce are home. If I'm going to be reverent about God's good earth, this is the place.

Until well into life, though, I never thought seriously about experiencing God's good earth in total isolation, at 20 degrees below zero. Some time ago it occurred to me that the time frame for that kind of experience was probably shrinking. The machines were getting more venturesome and the laws were changing.

So I stashed three days worth of food and fuel into a backpack, along with a small tent, a sleeping bag, an inflatable air mattress, and a paperback copy of Erica Jong's *Fear of Flying*.

To this I added a pair of skis, a full set of extra clothing for emergency, a battery-powered reading lamp, and for my pockets, a bottomless bag of trail food, the notorious *gorp*, much-beloved by the outdoor clans.

Thus encumbered, I skied into the thick Norway pines and spruce of the forest and lake country beyond the Echo Trail east of the town of Ely, where I was born.

I was alone. That was the provocation. This was not an experiment but a journey into a different consciousness. Most human beings shun isolation by instinct. So do I. But I thought: what would it take to create a day of absolute aloneness, in which you would see no other human being nor hear another voice?

The word "wilderness" can be misused in our casual conversation. Pure wilderness implies the absence of humans. What we call "wilderness" in America today is wild nature where humans tread occasionally. But if there is something truly close to wilderness in, say, the Minnesota in which I grew up, it is the northwoods in the dead of winter. It is the woods still free of both snowmobile or ski trail. It's the silences Sigurd Olson so revered, not for a minute or an hour, but for a day or more. Why not, I said. You can have wilderness without having to pretend it's Robinson Crusoe isolation. I wasn't marooned. Assuming I didn't break a leg or mistake Betelgeuse for the North Star, I could always ski the miles back to where I parked my car.

The few days that followed were unimaginable. There were no trails. I had a map and a compass. I could identify the frozen lakes and streams. What weren't mapped were the Indian pictographs that suddenly emerged across the basalt cliffs above the snow pack, spreading their faded burgundy and cornflower colors as a backlighting for the soundless firs. The characters in the pictograph seemed to be moving, an optical illusion created by the falling flakes. Locked into my skis I stared, barely breathing, trying to engrave the scene and my astonishment.

The day after my first campout I ran into a pack of wolves, romping on the ice of Home Lake, doing a lupine version of the games of horse we played on the basketball court. They must have been aware of the intruder. Probably they didn't care. The intruder moved out of range, still wondering, but moving with what the courts would call all deliberate speed.

It was cold, but I felt no discomfort. Skiing through the trackless woods put me in a kind of horizontal slalom course. The gates were the trunks of the big Norway pines. The downhill slalom riders had an advantage—they didn't have to watch for overhanging branches or dangling mats of grandfather's beard. It was strenuous, hauling that heavy pack, but exhilarating. You could plan a line through and around the Norways, lift your ski pole to dislodge a mini-avalanche of snow from the low branch, and absolutely frolic through the day. There were moments when I felt so free and rhapsodic that I'd sing gliding through the woods. And then I'd come out on a small lake shore and test each stride crossing the bay, alert to thin ice.

Once I heard a gurgling and stopped cold. The sound of running water is not a sound you can love while crossing a frozen lake. I twisted around in my skies, looking for the source of it and was relieved to spot a little brook running into the lake. I don't know why that particularly brook was still able to flow in the middle of winter but I wasn't overwhelmed by any urgency to find out. I headed for the nearest shore line and herringboned my way up the next hill.

At night the sleeping bag was warm, and the sounds around me mostly congenial. As the temperature dropped I could hear sap cracking in some of the surrounding trees, but that kind of northwoods percussion was familiar to me. I grew up in these parts, and as a child I listened to the same sound coming out of the roof of our house.

Late at night, with my skis speared upright in the snow to stake the tent, I would open the flap, gather the bottom of my sleeping bag in my hands and sort of walrus my way toward the opening. From there I could stare into the most unearthly of all spectacles in the night sky, the aurora borealis, shifting and shimmering in great streamers of greens and blues against the starlight. It was one of those rare and overpowering sights that you desperately wanted to share with someone. But no one else was here. And then I quietly switched gears mentally. The aurora borealis was here. I was here. The woods and the snow were here. That was the world tonight. Nothing intruded. And I began to think, "How marvelous, this." Otherwordly? No, not that. What was more natural? This was reality. A different world. Mine. But only a borrowed world, and only for a night or two. But I didn't need more.

I gathered my sleeping bag and slipped back into the tent.

On the next and last night, I found one final shaggy reality. It was New Year's Eve in the wildwoods, and I opened Erica Jong's raunchy *Fear of Flying*. I read for a half hour or so and started laughing noisily when the text got around to the more awkward grabbings and gropings. I would have sworn I heard sounds outside the tent but was too absorbed to check them out.

The next morning, I did the inspection. The snow around the tent was cluttered with large, hooved prints, too big for a deer or even two. My visitor was at least one very adult moose. The moose clearly had been attracted by howls inside the tent. It may have been a literary moose. Or it may simply have been a lonesome moose. I gave thanks that it wasn't a crabby moose, in which case both Erica Jong's prose and my anatomy would have been emphatically messed up.

I melted a couple of pounds of snow in my Svea camp cooker, made coffee, poured some dried oatmeal into the leftover water, added the remaining dregs of gorp, strapped my boots into my skies and headed back toward civilization.

My tracks were going to disappear in a few days. Maybe that wasn't soon enough. Leaving my campsite I was assaulted by the screeches of a handful of Canada jays, delivering some sort of commentary. I don't know the Canada jay vernacular and can't tell you their version of "Get lost." I didn't have much doubt about the general intent.

But I did take my time leaving.

A Changing Minnesota and
What We're Losing

March 2005

Nobel prize winners, social scientists and the nation's leading experts on government flocked to Minnesota years ago. They came to study what they called America's flagship state in providing public services, stimulating corporate growth and offering high quality of life for its citizens.

On the average, the public's bills for creating this kind of society were a little higher than what most of the other states assessed in state income taxes. What they bought was quality. It didn't matter whether the political movers were Democrats or Republicans. The citizens paid the bills the old fashioned way until the millennium rang in and the wave of the future took over in Washington. The new wave needed only a little more than a year to plunge the country into the red. The people running the government privately cheered. That was the idea. Give the surplus to the millionaires in tax cuts, the new wavers said. They would re-energize the great engine of corporate America. Let the schools and poor rubes go crying to the states. What happened was that the country went deeper into debt. The states, of course, were getting frozen out of money from the federal government. The plan was working. The public service scam would be shut down. A little later a war was invented. The government cut taxes for the millionaires again. The shelves were now bare and the states were clutching nickels.

In Minnesota a new governor came in with charm and sweet music for the taxpayers. Never, he said, would he ever tell the people of Minnesota they had to pay more taxes on his watch. It didn't matter if nattering nellies came to say the people are in trouble and the schools are desperate and health care is suffering.

I have a plan, said the governor and his new wave confederates. It will make Minnesota once more a shining star of civic and fiscal responsibility. We will gamble our way out of the deficit.

And the Legislature was soon immersed in a sea of thrilling new economic plans to restore Minnesota's status as a leader in governance. The owners of the biggest store in the country, the Mall of America, offered a plan to build a rooftop casino to attract an international clientele and the state would rake in. The governor's office responded with its own game, a partnership with Indian tribes who operate their own casinos in northern Minnesota but are hurting for customers. Whereupon the operators of the big Indian casino in suburban Minneapolis yelled foul, its big city gambling monopoly in jeopardy. So we then witnessed an expanding war between the Indian tribes while the state of Minnesota tried to broker a deal with the gambling industry and the tribes.

Whereupon the operators of the race track outside of Minneapolis said they wanted their own casino to sweeten the poker operation they run. At which point the bar owners of Minnesota came charging into the action for a bill that would put slot machines into thousands of liquor joints from border to border.

In the meantime, the metropolitan Minneapolis and St. Paul and suburbs, home to more than 2 ½ million people, was choking in traffic gridlock. Light rail had been brought in to provide some relief. But there wasn't enough money to expand public transit. So the governing body of the metropolitan district revealed a plan to cut service and increase fares to force low income people back into their automobiles, thereby expanding the gridlock.

This was happening, or threatening to happen, in a state that once gave America a model of how its citizens, its corporate strength, a creative government and its educational system could build a healthy society. It was a partnership that was unwritten but real.

There was a time when the state's political leaders concurred in how to measure the value of education and its priority. They then computed the costs. And for many years they agreed to pay the cost. If it meant raising taxes to provide responsible service, they raised taxes. Nobody was deported or excommunicated when it happened. Most of the tax raisers got re-elected. Service costs then weren't what they are now. The industrial mergers didn't dry up pensions as they do now. But what you did have in Minnesota government then was a willingness to look at the numbers honestly and to deal with them in ways the public understood. What you have today are charades, chasing after new money by pushing the state into widening layers of gambling, playing tribes against tribes as part of the political stakes, cutting off vulnerable people from health care to balance the budget and downgrading education.

The climate started changing when the self-described "taxpayers associations" began screaming that Minnesota taxes were driving industry out of the state and citizens into the poor house. The citizens didn't go into the poor house. And if some of the industries moved or put a branch operation into another state, the executives made sure they kept their homes in Minnesota, where their children could go to school and be treated in Minnesota hospitals.

I grew up in Minnesota, went to school in it, worked in it and have lived in it all of my more than 70 years, subtracting two years in the Army. I have prospered in it moderately, made my mistakes and a few scattered triumphs in it, and paid its taxes without storming walls to protest. Minnesota's medicine saved my life at least four times, bypass, cancer, carotid and more.

It has surrounded my life with extraordinary music, drama and art, with a creative industry and a humanitarian ethic so deep that it has survived even the whacky and destructive economics at the federal and state levels of government in the 21st Century. The state's devotion to its natural treasure has given me, and millions of others, woods, parks and waterways for a weekend or a lifetime. Its political leadership and its partnership with its citizens—when the state of Minnesota was at its best—lifted the condition of life in Minnesota to a place almost all of its people had reason to applaud. Its elected bodies often discarded partisanship to give a decent respect to the axioms of good and responsive government.

So what was this, some kind of jackpine paradise of modern living?

Well, no. But when Minnesota was at its best, it led the nation in creating the possibilities for a fulfilling life, for the lives of children to the lives of seniors and to the least in society. Its industrial leaders genuinely believed they had a responsibility to grow the community, not only because it sustained their profits but because it was right, or so it seemed to them. Somebody invented a term that later sounded cornball but actually had it in synch: "good corporate citizens."

Some of the corporate atmosphere changed with the onset of national corporate mergers that replaced the industrial families who created an ethic and solidarity that set Minnesota business apart in its relationship with its customers and the community—the Pillsburys, Daytons and the founders of Honeywell. The quality of its political leadership has moved from innovation and accountability to what we have had in the last few years: mimicry of the political and fiscal tricks that get by in Washington.

What we have now in America are federal tax-cutting policies and military spending splurges that shrink the states' ability to serve their people adequately. In most of the states, including Minnesota, this has led to the proliferation of innocuous-sounding "fees" that put an anvil on the backs of the lower middle class, the least able to pay them. The fees keep growing, often hidden in a morass of legal language. So do the actual taxes that punish addiction created by corporate advertising, such as cigarette taxes.

This is a caricature of good government. Minnesota, like most of the states around it, is now pitching ideas like state-run casinos and a sleek, modern political philosophy stuffed with denial. It runs like this: excuse the White House for its horrendous and often hidden military spending and its shameful tax cuts for the wealthy. But don't dare consider raising state taxes to pay for services the citizens need and schooling the children need more desperately. You can ignore paying for them by sliding the true cost into the future, pretty much forever.

The new creed gets worse. Never mind that those tax cuts strip billions of dollars from services for average and older Americans, and from schools. Those reductions literally will mean death for some of the victimized poor by giveaways to the already wealthy. That includes Minnesota. And if you run all of the branches of federal government, which means you also control the state budgets, you can play those marked cards indefinitely by keeping the public gullible enough or by suggesting that God approves. Paper the budget with dodges like bogus bookkeeping and funding shifts. And don't call that taxation, at least not until the next generation has to pay if it wants to avoid bankruptcy. And by that time the current guardians of the American dream will be safely out of reach of the voters.

This obviously is an invitation to eventual mediocrity. In Minnesota, it's a condition that has been partially delayed. The voters are still capable of seeing through the manipulation, as they did in the 2004 election when Minnesota not only voted against the Bush government but threw out 13 Republican legislators who didn't seem to be listening.

Why does the ethics of government and the trust of its citizens matter so much to a guy relatively comfortable in his 70s?

I was old enough in the 1930s to know how that mattered to the immigrants who poured into the Iron Range by the thousands more than a century ago. Most of them arrived scared and intimidated by the size and speed of America and its befuddling language. But not many of them turned back. The country's smokestack industries were expanding hot and impatiently. The corporate titans of steel had created a vast barony stretching from the iron mines of Minnesota and northern Wisconsin and Upper Michigan to the ore-melting furnaces of Indiana, Illinois and Pennsylvania. The Great Lakes swarmed with long and ungainly freighters hauling iron ore to the mills. The railroad and mining industries dispatched recruiters into the Balkans, Italy, and other Europe enclaves of disaffected workers and young families, offering modest inducements that would reward sweat and ambition.

In northern Minnesota men walked to the iron mines with their lunch buckets, sometimes more than two miles through snowdrifts and temperatures below zero. They strapped on flimsy helmets and carbide lamps, dug into the vermilion rock hundreds of feet below the surface, and did it gratefully. It was not a place for self-appointed martyrs. Nobody had to prod them into the steerage of the ships that brought them here. For a while my grandparents lived in bleak and scraggly mining settlements but eventually built their own homes and lived to send their children to school and to see their grandchildren in college.

It was the way America was supposed to work, and did. It's also why the new wave of migration to Minnesota, primarily Asian and Latino, can produce the same kind of cultural and economic enrichment for both the migrants and the state if its government acts with sensible vision, works with private industry sensibly and avoids tricking the books. But now we are concocting casino schemes to compensate for government timidity in being square with people.

One of the most moving moments in recent Minnesota history was the gathering of thousands to mourn the death of an industrialist and Republican political figure in 2004, Elmer L. Andersen, a former governor of Minnesota.

Of all of Minnesota's political leaders in the last half of the 20th century—and they included the transcendently popular Democrats, Hubert Humphrey, Walter Mondale, and Paul Wellstone—Elmer Andersen may have been the most respect-ed across all party lines. He represented the best of what had become a silent breed, the moderate Republicans who under-stood the strength of the partnership idea among rival political parties, the citizens and corporate Minnesota. It couldn't hap-pen every day, dramatically and significantly. It was closer to a state of mind. It depended crucially on the civil engagement of the players. Nobody expressed it more thoughtfully, or as unmistakably, than Elmer Andersen in his waning years.

He was still lucid and with a grip on how to govern that shamed the scrabbling for political gain that he was seeing in government today. In the last year of his life, he talked angrily about the shell games.

"People need quality services from government," he said, "and the way to provide them is through industrial development. Industrial development is built around education and investment in people, not tax cuts. Anyone who knows business knows that taxes are really not the issue that decides where firms locate. The crucial issue, after consideration of market, is the adequacy of the available work force. An industry surrounding new development goes where people are trained and skilled in that development. The firms that choose low tax states are those that can tolerate poor education because they rely on low-wage, unskilled labor... Paying taxes is like going to a store. You don't go to a store with the purpose of spending money. You go to obtain something you need or want. Taxes aren't a loss of money; they are the price of essential services...People need to be educated about government budgets, so they understand that tax money goes to services they want, and that if they don't pay the price they suffer."

This is truth, but it has a problem. People keep getting elected in America today by telling the voters: There IS such a thing as a free lunch if you want to live the good life.

By the time the citizens discover the truth they may be getting old, or whipsawed by the new slick economics. They may need help.

And it won't be there.

Iv. Africa Spins The Mind

The Preacher Faces a Lion, and Builds a Community

June 1998

The low cloud of the East African night sky scowled on the tossing savannah below it. To the Reverend David Simonson, sitting in a motionless Land Rover with a 16-bore shotgun in his lap, the sky looked hostile and perverse. He rued the absence of moon and stars. On most nights they were spectacular ornaments in the equatorial sky above the Maasai Steppes of Tanganyika. They had another virtue. They made it easier to see an approaching lion in the darkness.

Simonson had been in Africa more than a year preaching the word of God according to Martin Luther, but staring up at its blazing sky at night still filled him with wonder as it would a child. In starlight, the oceans of high grass and acacia trees that stretched off to the distant hills were engulfing, and the hills themselves seemed to lift to the limitless sky, creating a synergy that for the Reverend fused heaven and earth. God had to be in there somewhere. The stars lit the scene with the power and mystery of an Africa that he'd idealized back in the seminary, where he had committed himself to a lifetime as a missionary among the gaunt and elegant tribesmen called the Maasai.

But this night was not the sort to inspire such raptures. It wasn't normal. This night had no mystery or beauty for the young preacher from Minnesota. What it offered was a man-killing, cattle-killing lion. From the Land Rover, Simonson could hear the lion's spasmodic grunting, but the black night gave him cover. He tightened his grip on the stock of the shotgun. The preacher was trying to control his fear. It was not a grinding, unhinging fear. It crept up on him, the enveloping unknown. It was offset by an excitement he couldn't suppress. He had told the village's Maasai warriors to lie back while he went after the lion alone. It was the sensible thing to do, in the interests of both the Maasai and the preacher, precluding an accident that might turn the night into a disaster. He was secure in that decision. Still, the grunting and roaring rattled him. He knew it was not quite as near as it sounded, but God, it was near enough. The lion was somewhere out in the savannah beyond the village. The warriors stood by the thornbush hedges of their boma settlement, holding their spears while they looked out in the direction of the Land Rover. Some of them wanted the honor of going after the lion themelves. But they also knew that this lion was a killer. Every few minutes they would hear the booming sounds out there near the wells. Simba was prowling. They also knew that the preacher's shotgun was their best hope.

The Maasai scarcely knew this big young preacher with his black beard and wrestler's shoulders. He'd arrived in Naberera a few days earlier to get acquainted with the south Maasai district of the Lutheran Church of Tanganyika, where he was going to be the apprentice evangelist, replacing a pastor who had almost died trying to climb Kilimanjaro and was eager to return to the United States to recuperate.

The Maasai were aware that the new preacher had a shotgun. They also knew that the lion would be coming over the thornbush fence unless somebody stopped him. They had spears and, by the codes of the tribal culture, no fear of the lion. But by its behavior they were convinced that this was a crazed animal, and their spears were not going to protect their boma. Two nights earlier, with its mane streaming in the village torchlight, the lion entered the town and terrorized some school teachers near a shop, forcing them to flee into the church. At that point the lion had leaped through an open window of the church, routing the school teachers and temporarily staking out territory behind the organ. It was later determined that the beast had worn away its long teeth on its hunts, exposing the nerves and leaving it in constant pain, a rogue, deranged. In that state it had abandoned its normal prey of wildebeest and zebra and turned to humans and cattle. Both escaped the lion's first night rampage and also the second, when the villagers had taken refuge in the school. On the third afternoon the Maasai sent a delegation of *murran*, the warriors, to the mission cottage on the outskirts of Naberera, where Simonson was eating his supper of goat meat.

When the villagers arrived at the door of his hut Simonson stood, greeted them affably and offered them what he could of his meal. But the Maasai had come to recruit, not to eat. They were tall and solemn. With a mix of Swahili and Maasai language that Simonson figured out quickly, they asked the twenty-eight-year-old man of God—which is not quite the same as a man of peace—to help them kill the rampaging lion and save the village.

Simonson had been raised in Eastern Montana and South Dakota; he took his college education at Concordia College in Moorhead, Minnesota and later at Luther Theological Seminary in St. Paul. He had been a roughneck in his grade school days, and from adolescence to young adulthood an elbows-flying fullback and captain of the Concordia football team, as well as a pheasant and duck hunter. When he came to Africa he brought as much of his artillery—rifle, shotgun and pistol—as the British customs agents would allow. He hunted wildebeest and warthog with the other missionaries during his early months of mission training in the Pare Mountains of eastern Tanganyika and around Marangu off the slopes of Kilimanjaro.

But a warthog is not a charging lion in the lonely bush surrounding a Maasai boma. On this night, the homicidal lion and nearly a hundred miles of roadless nothing separated the young man of God from the shelter of the diocese of Arusha in northern Tanganyika.

Simonson sat quietly and briefly at his table to consider his options. The Maasai weren't there to socialize. Also, from some place in the distance they could hear the first guttural "hoof-hoofs," the unmistakable descending grunts of the approaching lion. Simonson knew enough about the habits of lions stalking a village. They usually came twice to terrify whatever was in sight or earshot. Reconnoitering, military people would call it. The third night they came to kill. They preceded the assault with ferocious sound effects calculated to freeze the victims into paralysis.

"He will come straight down the road tonight," they said. "He's going to jump over the thornbushes and come into the boma. We're going out to hunt him. Maybe you can head him off with your gun."

The preacher weighed his choices. 'On the one hand, if you kill it,' he reasoned to himself, 'you entrench yourself with the Maasai, or at least with this village tribe. After all, these people are going to be your parishioners if you ever make it in Tanganyika. You'll probably save some lives, too.'

A second possible outcome also loomed, however. He might miss. In fact, he might never get off a shot, or have too little time to reload! He might die. It was perhaps a more likely possibility than the first one. Simonson was a hunter, but only an amateur, and the lore of Africa was filled with sagas of Great White Hunters who had lost in similar showdowns and returned home in a sack. Simonson thought about that. He thought about Eunice and the kids back at Marangu. Perhaps he ought to tell the Maasai warriors that he had a wife and three kids back at Marangu and couldn't meet the lion tonight.

'Give them that answer,' Simonson told himself, 'and you may as well pack up and go back to preach in South Dakota. You're finished as a missionary. No Maasai from Naberera to the Serengeti is going to take you seriously when you talk about the brave Jesus Christ facing death to save humanity.'

It wasn't the way he had planned to start spreading the word of God, but no manual existed that could guide him on a decision like this. He sorted through the odds, attempting to apply reason to the situation, but the answer had already come. Simonson told the Maasai he would take his shotgun and go out to meet the lion.

The animal's roars were getting closer. He was suddenly gripped by the conviction that he ought to finish his meal. Maybe his body was telling him he needed all the protein he could get. Maybe it was some quirky mind game about a Last Supper. He asked the Maasai to wait outside, and he'd join them in a few minutes. When the meat was gone, he loaded his gun, put on his jacket, prayed briefly and went out to join the villagers.

I'll go alone, he told the Maasai. Although surprised, they respected his decision. The big preacher with his decisive movements and authoritative voice that filled up the house was something they hadn't expected. The Maasai aren't easily impressed by macho appearances. They are wary, tough, and pretty-well convinced that nobody can match their personal discipline and fearlessness. But this man was standing there with his shotgun and telling them to stay home; he was going after the lion himself.

Simonson explained it to a village school teacher before he headed toward the village outskirts in the Land Rover. "I don't want to get one of those guys shot if he gets into the line of fire."

The teacher nodded his understanding. A humanitarian, this preacher.

Well, yes and no. Simonson was convinced that the more people that were present during the encounter, the more likely one of them would get hurt or killed, either by the lion or by him. That was the humanitarian side. But there was another reason he wanted to go alone. He was riding out to face a killer lion. He was human and he was scared. But he also felt a rising thrill as the confrontation neared.

Dave Simonson was a mixed personality. Spreading the gospel in East Africa was part of his charter as a missionary. But there was much more. He and wife, Eunice, and their three children (two more would follow) were not going to be short-termers in Africa. The need for food, for schools and for medicine among the Maasai and the other tribes in Tanzania was overwhelming and heart-breaking. So he began with a commitment to serve those needs with all of his energy, and his considerable eloquence as an advocate often upgraded to his ferocity as an advocate. All of this came with a certain risk, and there were times when he invited it. Simonson was a man who was often motivated by risk as a goad to action. The appeal of it lubricated some of his behavior and attitudes. So, a lion was coming toward the village of a people he had vowed to befriend, to convert to Christianity and to heal. More than incidentally, the lion would also be coming toward David Simonson.

He checked the pump action of the shotgun. An old mission man back in Minnesota had strenuously argued the case for the 16-bore. "Everybody out there hunts with a 12-gauge," he said. "If you go with that, they're going to be bumming shells off you until you go dry."

He began to strategize as the Land Rover wheeled slowly toward the tawny grass outside the village. If the lion was coming to kill, he wasn't going to be skulking in the grass or ducking behind a tree. And true to form, Simonson could now hear him (as the Maasai villagers too had predicted) coming down the middle of the road, splitting the black night with his bellowing. The middle of that road outside Naberara was defined by a couple of ancient wells said to have been dug by the Phoenicians. Near the wells was a trough from which the Maasai women would haul the water in buckets or gourds to distribute among the cattle.

He felt his aloneness, heading slowly toward the wells. But he also felt a mounting excitement, hearing the lion, knowing it was there.

The headlights picked out something amber and hairy moving near the trough. The lights caught its eyes. The lion wasn't ducking. It was huge. It stood staring into the lights, throwing its head back, snarling. God, it was close. Twenty feet at the most. Simonson felt a shiver inside. Freeing the gun's safety, he got out of the Land Rover and stood behind the headlights. For a moment, he was conscious of his sensations. He was scared and electrified, charged with adrenaline. It surged through him like floodwater, making him bigger and lusting to go one-on-one with this killer beast in front of him. He was a minister of God, but at this very moment he was indivisibly and gloriously a hunter, and this was the trial he had never envisioned. How was he going to deny the thrill of it? The adrenaline was eating him up. Inwardly he was yelling at the lion as he put the stock to his shoulder. "All right, Simba. Let's go." He'd never experienced the naked power of these colliding emotions, the excitement, the tension, the escalating drive of combat melting the fear. It was almost an out-of-body experience, the hard and reflexive current that propelled the shotgun to his shoulder.

He fired.

The charge hit the lion squarely and flung him backwards. He flashed his teeth, thundered his fury and pain and started to get up.

Simonson shot again. The lion slumped, dead. Simonson stared, struggling to comprehend. Then he flung himself to his knees in the soft earth and bawled. "Thank you, God." And then he was crying and laughing, liberated from the domineering tension of this bizarre encounter. Within minutes he was surrounded by spear-waving Maasai warriors, declaring their gratitude and their respect—perhaps their amazement—for the black-bearded preacher who went out to face the lion alone, and brought him down.

It was an initiation into a brotherhood—the young missionary couple and the Africans—that would last a lifetime. It was the beginning of a ministry that would heal thousands of Africans and build schools for thousands of children who until then had to read and write in the merciless sun or behind rocks or in the thornbushes. It was a ministry that brought the saga and gospel of Jesus Christ into the lives of more thousands. Some of them reacted to Christianity with exuberance and some with bafflement, in the normal proportions of tribal converts. But it was also a ministry that would unite the Africans with large numbers of Americans whose consciences were aroused by Simonson's relentless appeals for money to save the lives and educate the kids of people he now called his brothers and, considerably later, his sisters. Simonson's swashbuckling style didn't achieve unanimously giddy reviews from his superiors and some of his colleagues. His obsessions and commitments, his spasms of ego and impatience, his raw visibility as a bigger-than-life character on the mission frontier, brought him into conflict with church authorities and peers. They got him into quarrels with accountants, led to a four-year exile at the hands of an African bishop and forced him into hospitals for by-pass surgery, anthrax, malaria, cancer and diabetes. He was almost killed in a plane crash in his final years of mission. Later, after his retirement, he suffered a stroke that almost destroyed his power of speech.

Somehow he overcame and endured. While his missionary energies converted several thousand of the Maasai to Christianity, he and Eunice were fundamentally healers, teachers and friends of the Africans they served. Each day for years Eunice nourished and comforted African women of the nearby villages who would come to their home for medicines she kept in her kitchen cabinets for them. Sometimes all she had was an embrace. They loved her and called her "mama." Her husband was essentially unstoppable. He raised millions of dollars from American churches, from foundations, corporations, wealthy donors and from service clubs in America and Europe. With that money he built 2,500 one room schoolrooms in Africa, a clinic in Tanzania that saved hundreds of lives, and a secondary school for Maasai girls to reverse hundreds of years of suppression of women in the Maasai society. It's impossible to estimate the number of Africans who are alive today but would have died of malnutrition or sickness or simple neglect without the intervention of David Simonson in the 50 years he and his wife worked in Africa. He carried his faith—and it was unbreakable—wherever he went. And whenever it was prudent in the African bush, he also carried his shotgun.

II.

I walked with David Simonson in the Great African Rift one summer. Hiking in the Rift tends to give you perspectives on life and the dimensions of time and nature that I'd never experienced climbing a mountain in the Andes or skiing alone through the winter wilderness. Six of us walked 200 miles of this vast gorge of more than 4,000 miles to raise money for the one-room primary schools the reverend's Operation Bootstrap was building in Tanzania. He conceived an eight-day walk through the volcanic ravines and the savannahs to generate visibility for his fund drive. He conscripted hikers from people he considered easy marks for those goals. I fell into that category.

So we began the walk to Arusha from Loliondo, through country that led later into the land of the Maasai but first to the Sonjo, who still used bows and poison-tipped arrows to hunt cattle thieves. Two feet of volcanic dust caked the trail. It rimmed the great and mysterious alkaline lake of Natron at the base of the still-active volcano of Oldonya Lengai and took us into lion country. Africa was almost buried in poverty, AIDS and corruption then as it is today. But there are more

Africas then the Africa of sickness and wars, and there are Africas for the future. For me it came to one constant. The Africa of today. And how do you define it? I've been there a dozen times and can barely presume to begin. It's bewildering and almost helpless in its sickness and hunger and poverty but magnificent in its raw nature. Its future is in those dark faces that can so easily be transformed by some act of recognition. Africa elusive. Africa cruel. Africa that burns its way into the living soul of those who want to possess it but know they cannot. Africa of the women's orange and black saris, walking upright at a slow-march, carrying gourds of water on their heads but moving searchingly into a new time when they may walk with their heads free to the air.

There is the Africa of the plain, with its butter yellow grass waving in the wind; the Africa of the desert and the great Nile, Lake Victoria, and Kilimanjaro. There is the Africa of Karen Blixen and David Livingstone—an Africa both idyllic and murderous, with sick, hungry kids, gorgeous landscapes, and herds of wildebeest. And there is the Africa that Aadje Geertsema watches for hours from her chair beside the fire. She runs a safari lodge at Lake Ndutu and she has been there for more than twenty-five years, but she is still transfixed to see the day giving way to the spreading vermilion and indigo of the African twilight. There are hundreds of Africas, most of them still searching, a lot of them still fighting, millions dying before their time.

It might have been this searching and implausible Africa, so wild and electric, that unfolded in our walk with Simonson in the Rift under the equatorial sun.

We got up in the darkness to walk the day's twenty-five miles, and we were well into the trek, when we heard the first lion at 5:30 a.m.

It was a few hundred feet away. It was growling and bellowing. I couldn't resist the thought that it was lonely. The confirmation was an answering call from a second lion a few hundred feet on the other side of our trail. The lions had us straddled, and we could only guess at the significance of the grunts and roars they were exchanging across the tall grass of the Engaruku Basin. The reverend was carrying two Ruger Blackhawk .357 revolvers in his holster. They looked impressive, but if the reverend was going to save us from a charging lion with a .357 revolver, we had a better chance quoting from John 3:16. I will tell you this about the roar of a lion when it is close and

all that stands between you and the lions are a few yards of blowing grass and a $14 flashlight from Target: I have heard approaching freight trains when my car neared a crossing. I have heard 10-ton boulders falling from a mountain cliff overhead, and I have heard lightning bolts splitting nearby trees in the Minnesota wilderness, and I prefer any of those convulsive sounds to the sound of a roaring lion in the African bush. It is a sound that cuts through your bones and spins your stomach. When it is truly close, it seems to shake the ground under you.

But by sunrise the lions were gone and the reverend, never dazzled by long sermons, led a two-minute devotional before we were off for Sonjo Country. There, the friends and parishioners of Simonson—his converts—were scurrying through the forests, their bodies striped with white paint, a bow and poisoned arrows in their hands. They weren't looking for us, thank God. They were after Maasai cattle rustlers who'd just raided their pasture. Simonson introduced us to one of his favorites, a little guy with a huge bow and enough toxin in those arrows to paralyze a regiment.

I thought then: You aren't going to meet many people like David Simonson. I wasn't sure Christendom is ready for it. He was beefy, gregarious and devout. He was also a passable autocrat and showman, taking us through his East Africa, introducing us to the scores of natives who knew him, some of whom he'd baptized. And a few miles later we were immersed in something marvelously alien and primeval. Monkeys called down and seemed to be mocking us, unseen in branches so dense they sealed out the sun. Wild primrose crowded our trail. A family of guinea hens flitted for cover ahead of us.

As we hiked along through this East African wilderness of acacia and fever trees and elephant grass, between the purple escarpments of the great Rift, I began to ask myself, Is it essentially any different from a thousand years ago?

Yes and no. The wilderness was almost the same. Those sounds in it, the screams of one animal yielding to the superior strength of another, were about the same.

But the revolver-packing preacher up ahead, Simonson, made it different. He wore his white beard and western boots and Outback hat. He had vast shoulders and a bountiful gut, and he waddled a little when he walked. We walked with him not only because his Africa was an irresistible Africa but because Simonson was a special kind of dreamer, with his Bible in his belt and the Rugers on his hips, but a dreamer still. He saw African babies who deserved something more in their lives than malaria and lung disease. We entered low scrubland as we came out of the Rift. The wind created spiraling dust rising hundreds of feet in the air, transforming itself into moving walls of silt that turned day into dirty brown. We lunched in the dust-filled classroom of a stone schoolhouse the Canadians built four years ago. A pupil's notebook was lying on a bare bench that served as a desk. In carefully crafted letters, the Maasai boy had made notes about how to write a letter in English. And now this same boy was somewhere on the great plain, standing watch over a herd of cattle as his ancestors had done for hundreds of years.

With a Maasai school teacher acting as guide, we scaled the 800-foot escarpment and came out on a wide meadow where herds of goats and cattle grazed. Mountains rose in all directions. It was the kind of scene you might experience in central Montana, except that here there was the inferno of the desert gorge just behind us, the snows of Kilimanjaro to the east, thatched villages just above us, and giraffe, gazelles, ostrich and hyena not many miles away. Add roaring lions. It was hard for the brain to take it all in.

In the final hours, Africa gave us a mural of its startling geography, its pain, history and hypnotic force. The palisades separating us from Arusha lifted before us. The walk had been demanding and overwhelming. But when we arrived on the outskirts of Arusha, 200 miles and eight days from where we had started, we walked beneath groves of bougainvillea and flame trees. It was one more Africa. A tribal medicine man we met explained it: if you dream enough, the beauty in Africa outlasts the pain.

The Faces of the Nile

November 2003

When Agatha Christie sipped tea on a hotel terrace above the Nile and concocted her fictional schemes of murder most vile nearly a century ago, the character of the river was an inseparable part of the plot.

The Nile was then, and had been for a few hundred eons, the headstrong goddess of Africa's mighty and mysterious wild nature. The Nile was the keeper of Africa's secrets and, more maternally, Egypt's secrets. As a force of nature, flowing unencumbered for thousands of miles, it was free and glorious, haughty and basically unmanageable.

By the time I first saw the Nile in the 1990s, its impetuous surge through the Sahara in Egypt had been curbed by the massive high dam south of Aswan. The goddess river had been industrialized to bring electricity to millions who'd never known it, and harvests of corn and bananas to hundreds of miles of desert that were once lifeless.

But beyond time and change, it is still the Nile, the nurturer of humanity and a wellspring of our art and science. More than any phenomenon of nature I've known in my travels, it links the then-and-now of our earth. Its currents rise in the jungle and sweep for 4,000 miles and three months through wilderness and desert to the Mediterranean. They reach into the deepest antiquity of Africa. And somehow that history, locked for centuries in tombs and hieroglyphs, becomes relevant in the psyche of the stunned western visitor who might have arrived in the desert a few days before with a head cluttered by high tech gobbledygook.

In the times I've seen it and felt the river's history, it has always stopped me in my tracks. The Nile brings to the traveler more than its power to evoke another age. Sometimes, especially at night when it's kindled by starlight, it is simply a thing of loveliness. You can fall into a trance watching it, trying to transport yourself into the time of who? Ramses II?

You think: Dynasties ago, the pharaohs invoked the Nile to seal their immortality. You think further: Thousands of years later the engineers poured mountains of dirt and concrete where pharaohs feared to tread, built the largest man-made lake on earth, flooded the lands of the Nubians—and made the Nile a little more manageable.

But in the heart of a roamer, it remains the irresistible river of the ages. Now that I have seen both the culmination of the Nile, where it joins the sea, and its source, where it charges fully-grown out of the very soul of Africa at Lake Victoria, I find it difficult to leave it when it is at its most alluring.

At Aswan, the Nile flows silken out of the cataracts and then beneath the garden terrace of the Old Cataract Hotel where Agatha Christie plotted the lively homicidal conspiracies that were left to the redoubtable Hercule Poirot to unravel without fail. When I travel in Egypt, I usually set aside a couple of hours in Aswan to make a pilgrimage to the spot where Agatha did some of her writing and much of the work for *Death on the Nile*. The Sofitel chain now operates the Cataract, which is probably a gift to the Christie faithful. It could have been reincarnated as one more museum, which Egypt could probably do without. The old hotel's dark-wooded dignity has been scrupulously preserved. So have the courteous whispers with which a greeter from the staff confronts the visitor. The rest of my small and inquisitive group had left for the day to visit the Philae Temple, which had survived the river's reconfigurations thirty years ago. We'd cruised for three days on the Nile, and were scheduled to leave Aswan for the Pyramids and Cairo the next day. I'd seen the Philae three times and was politely excused by the others.

When I arrived at the hotel I was surprised to find that the gatekeeper at the entrance to the botanical gardens had been replaced. I got acquainted with the old gatekeeper during my previous visits. In fact, he was onto me the minute I first appeared there ten years ago. On that first visit, he had asked if I was guest at the hotel. I didn't say yes. What I did was to shrug ambiguously. He took this to mean I wasn't. If you weren't a guest you probably had to pay to visit. That was going to take the charm out of the whole episode. I looked at the gatekeeper with my best face of the abandoned waif. He smiled benevolently and welcomed me to the Old Cataract with a gracious bow. In the years afterward we actually became friends. It became a tradition.

But the young man who had replaced him held a small packet of vouchers in his hand, explaining that visitors were welcome to the Old Cataract with a minimal $5 purchase in restaurant fare. So much for tradition. But I thought this was a reasonable tradeoff for the loss of my old equity. The lobby's historic muted gloom and stuffed furnishings were reverently untouched by the new management. I threaded my way through yards of unoccupied armchairs and onto the terrace for spiced tea.

The tea had to wait.

The terrace opened on a stunning eruption of color and exotica, a mural out of *Scheherazade*. Spunky little sailboats, the feluccas, bounced and glided in the distance off Elephantine Island and kids splashed after them in their tiny dinghies, rowing with their hands, trying to catch up. Beneath the terrace spread an arbor of hyacinths and palms, and beyond it the Nile leaped in frothy cascades, more a ballet than a cataract, after which the river broadened and resumed its quiet elegance. It was the kind of interlude you wanted to engrave.

To international politicians, Egypt is maddening and disappointing; with the right kind of leadership it might be part of the solution to the deadly turmoil of the Middle East. For the historian, what is important about Egypt ended two thousand years ago. For the social developer, Egypt's reluctance to explore the rewards of modernity is depressing. But for the visitor open to different faces and different tongues, it's a lark to walk through the cluttered local shops of Luxor, to banter with the peddlers, and to watch with wide eyes as the daily fast of Ramadan ends with the rays of the sun, and place settings for twelve or twenty-four suddenly appear in the streets as the all-night feast commences.

On our last night in Cairo Susan and I walked along the Nile for an hour in the gloaming. So here was the eternal river, flowing beside us in the midst of an enormous city of twenty million. The urban chaos had pretty much subsided for the day. We walked past towering western hotels with glass fronts, beneath graceful mosque domes and minarets only a block removed from shabby apartment buildings. Wealth and poverty commingled; east and west were awkwardly paired and the news of a hotel bombing in Istanbul, Turkey, was fresh and ugly. The constant in all of this was the Nile. It almost invited some kind of interrogation. How many generations of humanity had it silently witnessed and how much suffering? The river tonight wasn't saying. It couldn't talk but it could reflect.

Oddly, we heard a voice. It came from the sidewalk, not the river. "My friend," the horseman said. "I have carriage. You tired."

"We're not; we're talking to the river," I said brightly.

"That mean you *really* tired," he said.

We walked 50 yards further, and called back to the horseman.

"You right. We tired."

So we rode a horse-drawn carriage through a multi-million dollar tunnel built for high-speed traffic in the middle of Cairo, and waved to a donkey rider who was doing the same thing.

Some of the marvels of Egypt are not so ancient.

Coming Down from Kilimanjaro
with a Heavy Mind

August 2002

It wasn't the most cordial place for reviewing a lifetime fixation, my own. This was Kilimanjaro, one more time.

I climbed into the African night, trying to appease my lungs and aching calves. The Southern Cross hung over my right shoulder and the sky was a bonfire. But I was in no mood to appreciate the splendor. Kilimanjaro was a grind, again. Still, I couldn't get enough of it.

My mind sorted through the memories of more than forty years of climbing and clambering on the edge, trying to make sense of both my fatigue and this extravagant outpouring of energy, in my seventy-second year, climbing one more mountain.

The physical exertion was compounded by the cross-examination I had going. It was provoked by the realization that this was probably the last climb I would ever make, after nearly a hundred of them. That fact wasn't going to do much to disrupt the course of history but it might be comforting to my next of kin. The more I thought about it the more stubbornly I prodded myself and I almost said it aloud: "Lay it out so that at least *you* understand it. What are you doing on this mountain at your age and is there any intrinsic justification for it beyond needing to get to the top one more time?"

The debate pretty much ended right there. Why did I need any other reason to be on Kilimanjaro?

But I knew there were more.

When I was young, mountaineering and rock climbing were an alien world to most Americans. Today, the epics on Everest are best-sellers in America and absorb millions through the adventure and history channels. Hundreds of thousands of American youngsters learn climbing techniques as school electives. Four-year-olds know about belays.

And yet when climbing comes up at the socials, and the questions are asked, most people who climb recreationally shrink from giving a protracted monologue, uncomfortable at the thought of drifting into theatric accounts of their experiences. So the answer to the question, "What's it like?" usually will produce less than a blinding revelation.

I got into trouble once with my well-intended response that began: "One thing that can happen on a hard climb is that you might find out what you really have in you."

My interrogater asked the obvious question: "Well, what have you got in you?" which led me down into a bottomless swamp of self-analysis, murky enough to drive a clinical psychologist to the wall.

Yet a thousand feet from the summit in the equatorial darkness of Kilimanjaro, I found myself asking: "All right, what has all this striving and exertion done to you and for you?"

You have time to explore those psychological mine fields on Kilimanjaro because the mountain presents no serious technical problems. It lifts you to the edge of the stratosphere, and you're usually bouldering your way toward the summit in the coldest part of the night, a schedule that gives you some time and space on the descent. There are no crevasses to bridge on Kilimanjaro and no perpendicular walls to claw. For me, the "why" of climbing is fascinating stuff but too often unfulfilling because you get lost separating the real reasons from the melodramatic ones. In the end, the answer for me was pretty straightforward. As a kid, I was excited by alpine photos on the classroom walls and by the mountaineering sagas I read in the library. As a kid I climbed trees, because it's what kids do. As I grew up my curiosities turned the trees into mountains. I had idealized the high country from those stories of triumph and tragedy. The mountains seemed both an arena and a high altitude Nirvana that rewarded those who were willing to take them on. I later walked beneath the Matterhorn, on leave from the Army, and on my first visit to the American West I learned the rudiments of climbing.

The shock came early. On my early attempts in the Grand Tetons of Wyoming I was devastated to discover that climbing on an actual mountain threw me into spasms of terror, nearly froze me. I could hear the guide above me, calling instructions. I couldn't see him. I dug my fingers into a seam of the granite wall at 11,000 feet and had to fight off a rising panic. The rope tightened against my ribs. The wind screamed in my ears and flung the uncoiled rope in front me into writhing loops and contortions. I was alone on a 60 degree flake of cold and inhospitable stone. I yelled for more tension on the rope. The guide yelled back. "You've got all there is."

When I reached him, he peered at me, puzzled and amused but not unkind. "It's really not that ferocious," he said. "Trust the rope. It's like anything else. This is an unknown for you. It tends to shake you up, like any unknown."

I learned. I learned how to manage the rope and the technique of climbing on rock, ice and snow. I began to enjoy. My skills matured. I could lead a climb in the Alps. I climbed frozen waterfalls and snow mountains in the Andes and the Himalaya; and in time the camaraderie of it joined the glorious atmospherics of the high world: the first rays of the sun touching our faces, Gottlieb's and mine, on the summit of the Matterhorn; a distant chiming of the church bells in the village of Zermatt; the sight of a tiny colony of gingerbread houses in Grindelwald thousands of feet below the Mitteleggi Ridge of the Eiger; the west wind cracking our cheeks above the crater of Ranier; and the tinkling of my ice ax on the glacier in the pre-dawn darkness approaching Mt. Owen in the Tetons.

They were scenes and sounds to last a lifetime, filtered through the thin air of this remote world we had shared. They would re-unite me in spirit, year after year, with the faces of the men and women who had come into my life in the mountains, some for a day, some now gone. It is a powerful but capricious world, benign in its warmth and invitation today, savage in the violence of its thunderstorms tomorrow.

And I loved each day of it.

The darker side of the experience? The risk? Was that part of the allure of climbing too? It was a question I sifted out on Kilimanjaro.

It was and is. But you have to be careful how you put it. Eventually somebody is going to talk about death wishes and daredevil urges, and that isn't really what sensible climbing is about. So if not that, what then?

A manageable risk? Reducing the odds by understanding one's capabilities and limits? Yes, that. By preparing. By knowing that pride often does go before a fall. By knowing the others on the rope and having confidence in them. Being aware of the weather. All of that lessens the risk of trouble on the mountain. Yet moving upward on an exposed, high-angle cliff, testing the holds, putting the body's weight on a two-inch lip in the mountain face—all of that revs the adrenaline to a pitch not available in the usual ramblings of life.

The risk, of course, is self-imposed. The mountain is real, but inanimate. It is rock and ice. It is also neutral in whatever crisis evolves in the attempts to climb it. Climbing it is a problem to be solved, created by the climber. That is the simple equation of climbing. The climber doesn't *have* to climb the mountain in the way the smugglers did in the Alps or as refugees do today in the Himalayas to escape political oppression or in fact to escape murder. Climbing a mountain for the simple pleasure or for adventure—man-facing-nature as a test of stamina and will—is a relatively new phenomenon in human culture.

But its appeal as a kind of high altitude testosterone shot tended to vanish after my early days of climbing. It wasn't so much the onset of a new sensitivity, but that the earlier ideas of combat had given way to a comfort level—comfort with my abilities to climb well and with endurance, and with my reflexes when danger came. It meant I could open my eyes to the gifts of this new and spectacular dominion I had found, a kind of solidarity with the wind and the heights, the sun and the sky.

There is an almost irresistible impulse to ascribe human qualities to forces of nature such the mountains. I've done it here. We pretend that mountains can be benevolent or elegant, brutal or furious. We speak of them as if they exerted a will of their own. The mountain is none of this. And yet the imagination can capture the mind so completely that when you rest on one of the stone benches beside the trail in the Himalayas, you may let yourself drift into a reverie as you contemplate the scene above you. The mountain's fluted ice fields flash diamonds in the late afternoon sun, and the mountain can become a chalice in the sky. For a moment that is a reality more than a metaphor. It is exactly the way I picture the most beautiful mountain I've ever seen, Machapuchare in the Himalayas. The Hindus call it sacred. Why not? Its twin peaks rise high above an encircling ruff of clouds, as though held by unseen hands.

A chalice.

So most of the climbs of my later years were closer to pilgrimages. Something better replaced the guts-and-glory part of it. Climbing then became going high in familiar places, feeling airy and free, smelling the aroma of the rock, knowing the craft, climbing with friends who saw it the same way.

Now, for the last time, I was crabbing my way up toward the summit of this celebrated mountain, Kilimanjaro. Hemingway wrote of the riddle of the leopard whose remains were found just below the summit. What was this predatory animal of the savannah doing more than four miles above the sea? The leopard was real. That was not part of the fiction. The story seemed to deepen the mysteries of Kilimanjaro, its silent witness to the inhumanity of the slave trade of not so long ago, the receding ice fields, its volcanic history. It has become its own legend and part of it actually seems unearthly. The first lunar astronauts trained on its higher reaches to condition themselves psychologically for the moonscape they would find on their historic flight.

The trail got steeper as we neared 17,000 feet. Kilimanjaro doesn't require acrobatics on ice and rock cliffs. You don't need a rope for protection. The climb consists of slogging on loose volcanic scree with a headlamp on your helmet and not enough water in your pack. But it is a great mountain just the same, filled with history, and it is worth the grind.

We stopped. The guide, David, a Tanzanian and a friend from earlier climbs, lit a cigarette. I rested on a boulder and threaded the memories. Kilimanjaro now five times, the Matterhorn eight times, the Grand Teton seven times, Huascaran, the Eiger, all the others. I thought about the goal-setting, the glumness on days when I had to turn back. Were those failures? And I told my brain: "Enough. If this is the last mountain climb, be kind to yourself. Remember all that was so great about it."

I did. The first streaks of violet began lighting the sky above Kilimanjaro. We were close to 18,000 feet. David wanted to take five to talk with a buddy who was coming down. I wanted five to put out the fire in my three broken ribs from an accidental episode on the New York subway five days before. We stopped.

Later I recalled the sensations of that night on Kilimanjaro because they represent a watershed for me in how I look at myself, and at life, after all those years of walking the edge. I had climbed this mountain four times before, from 6,000 feet to 19,000 feet and back to 6,000 feet, once almost idiotically in 2 ½ days because of a compressed schedule. But on this night I was nearly wiping out at 17,000 feet. It wasn't so much my age, although it would have been silly to discount that factor. Nor could I discount what had happened to me in New York. At a clinic in Minneapolis a few days after the accident, a doctor handed me a chest wrap and said "you can climb Kilimanjaro without risking any more injury to your body, but you're probably going to learn things about your pain threshold you never thought about before."

I didn't really feel much pain on Kilimanjaro. What I felt was imminent strangulation. The chest wrap, tight and implacable under my sweater and jacket, made breathing at three miles in the sky a continuing horror. I told David to stop and I'd pull it off. I couldn't see David's face in the dead of night but I knew what it was registering. David was an aging veteran of Kilimanjaro climbing, nearing 55. He wore a short-brimmed Greek sailing cap and a look of eternal weariness. His face was an unfailing picture of wry fatalism and a total absence of anxiety, as though he was never going to be surprised by anything he saw on Kilimanjaro. So here was his old pal from the USA peeling off his chest wrap at more than 17,000 feet. David didn't know much about broken ribs except that they usually hurt like hell if they didn't get some support. What he wanted most at that moment was (a) to show reasonable sympathy and (b) to get going. He tapped me on the top of my wool cap. Sympathy. And he started moving again. I could breathe better, the ribs hurt but we were moving.

We went toward the top together, and now we were there. David was whistling some native tune, and on the summit ridge I did a mock dance. We hugged and shook hands and my eyes started to fog up. David figured it probably wasn't the wind.

We descended through the sudden heat of the midmorning and through the mists of dust flung up by others ahead of us. I knew the camp attendants were going to meet us with jugs of orange juice before we disappeared into the Kibo Hut for an hour of sleep, and then six more hours of climbing down to the Horombu Hut at 12,000 feet.

The years ahead confirmed that it was my farewell to high mountain climbing. The mountain experience certainly didn't end. There were high treks to come in the Himalayas and the land of the Incas in Peru. But the adrenaline of the nights before the summit climbs has been banked, and months later—not immediately—I felt no regrets.

Mountains don't give you approval. They can give you direction, and sometimes they can tell you where you went right or wrong with a piece of your life that had to do with expectations, understanding of self, the need to share a burden, and the simple grace of humility. I thought of that on the descent and remembered a tidy little maxim from AA: "Humility is not thinking less of yourself, but thinking of yourself less." Coming down one last time, you can examine the successes, on mountains and in the experiences of life. And you can tell yourself that reasonable preparation for a legitimate goal, with sensible behavior, can get you there. And there was a final benediction on this descent from Kilimanjaro. A thanksgiving was in order: for all of those marvelous sounds of the high world, the yodels above the Mosley cliffs on the Matterhorn, the roar of the hurricane winds against the tent walls in the Andes and the Himalayas and the whistling in the ears when we glissaded down the snowfields of the Grand Tetons. Thanks for the silence on the summit of the Eiger and for the sunrise over the Weisshorn; for Glenn Exum's smile on his last climb of the Grand, and for the solemn hand of my partner Rod Wilson when the rope held and saved our lives in the Andes.

And finally, thanks for those fleeting moments when our hearts could race with the wind and reach for the sun.

V. Life in Today's Arena: Helmets and Stock Options

Billion Dollar Football—A Goliath Running Amuck

November 2000

The Golden Boy, Paul Hornung, abdicated years ago as the resident Adonis of pro football. He did that with heartfelt reluctance. If you were once the prince of the night parlors around the National Football League, you don't give up that exalted status without regret.

But here he was, back on camera in a TV studio with white locks flowing and an impressive gut, recycled as a sage and ancient mariner of pro football.

The issue of the hour was the impact of megabucks on the pro football game Hornung once revered. Never mind his reputation as one of its ranking after-hours rascals when he played. Hornung's code on the field was hard and uncompromising. He played each down faithful to the code. The men he respected on both sides of the line played the same way. Later, at the reunions, they laughed at some of the slogans. Guts and all. Going to the wall. But they played the game by those hairy axioms. The question: Did today's boys of autumn, watching the stock markets as avidly as the Monday morning stats, pound the line as ferociously and party together as exuberantly as the musketeers of pro football's greening years in Hornung's time. Did they feel the same loyalty?

So here was a pro football Hall of Famer, Hornung, a Heisman Trophy winner, broadcaster and retired boulevardier, now in his mid-60s. He was conscripted by the cable channel to tell us where the colossus of pro football was going in the new millennium, and how it got to be so rich and vulgar.

He passed the first and only true test of the designated sage.

He admitted that he didn't know how pro football got to be so rich and vulgar.

But he knows it is. And because of that he grieved about it, he said, along with a few thousand other old pros. Although he was a marvelous and hard-willed player on the field, and a

scamp with some impressive appetites off it, hypocrisy never seemed to be part of his toolkit. I always liked him for that. And true to form, he was now mourning pro football's fixation with big money, while admitting that he really didn't know if he would act any differently in the same circumstances.

What he meant was that if the money was there and if it meant dumping the team he was playing for to get it, he'd probably go after the dough.

He had been loyal to the Packers and Fuzzy Thurston and Vince Lombardi in the 1960s, he seemed to be saying. But would he be professing the same love for the frozen streets of Green Bay and Speed's Bar if he was a free agent in the year 2000, and Jerry Jones in Dallas was on the horn and saying, "hot damn, Paulie, how about 25 mill for four years and a $12 mill signing bonus?"

Yet what seemed to bother him more than the appearance of a whole new breed of gypsy millionaires was the effect their appearance had on the emotional side of the game he remembered—the days in Green Bay, Lombardi's scowl, lining up with Jim Taylor, roughhousing in the locker room with Hawg Hanner, Jerry Kramer and Willie Davis.

On this particular day, Hornung was the fifth or sixth of the old pro lions to make an appearance on the sports channels. Today's sports television can't get enough of the embattled old faces and the marquee names, which dress up a half hour show and give it credibility.

In television's obsession with pro football today, this is a benign and handy fate that eventually overtakes most old pros who are glib or whose fame has a long shelf life. We should applaud. Everyone wants to feel needed but not everybody gets reincarnated on national television after being washed out of the business years ago. A lot of these people are my old pals. They are the used-up heroes of the football industry, some of them still relatively famous and prosperous, some of them gimping along on the pension plan's margins.

Forty years ago they might have been pumping gas as a career change. Today they are pursued by TV producers who want to make the next 30 minutes sound fresh and opinionated and, with luck, a little outrageous. TV prowls the phone books and casting offices for them. Sometimes it tries the nursing homes. Television's saturation of America with pro football today is ruthless. The NFL itself is narcissistic. It will have its own TV network soon, joining its other idolaters. The game seems compelling to enough Americans to push TV into 24-hour a day coverage. No relief is granted. If you turn on the set, television takes no prisoners and grants no escape. From September to February it is wall to wall football. If you turn off the television set it's there on Internet and a thousand web sites. If you click off the Internet it's in the morning paper—profiles, posters, and a crazy, virtual reality football game created from cyberspace. If that's not enough, you get one more quote from a belligerent cornerback who knows how to stop the generally unstoppable Randy Moss.

It ought to be noted that in the menagerie of millionaire novelty acts in pro football, Moss occupies his own privatized theater. The majority of them are relentless self-promoters featuring end zone contortions and noisy extortions demanding more forward passes and attention. Moss, on the other hand, is no grandstander, at least not 24/7. He compensates by acting like a moody and self-absorbed adolescent who happens to be one of the spectacular talents in pro football.

All of this round-the-clock football chatter and occasional hysteria is a million dollars worth of free advertising for pro football on TV and in the newspapers, as well as for the peddlers who push team merchandise. But the newspaper doesn't look at it that way. The appeal of pro football is so broad and deep, it will say, the hysteria so widespread that the public's appetite *cannot* be fully fed. And unless the newspaper is out in front of the hysteria, it will be dumped into the ditch of irrelevance by its media competitors. So it does 12-page special supplements for Game Day. Hundreds of thousands of newspaper readers can't possibly read them to the end. But they do.

There were other faces and voices on the show where Paul Hornung was a guest. But Hornung's face and voice were the ones that drew me. It wasn't so much that we were acquainted, first when he played for the Packers and I wrote pro football for the Minneapolis newspaper. Later we had endless gab sessions in the hotel coffee shops and bars in his years as a broadcast analyst covering the Vikings. No, what attracted me to Hornung's testimony on that show was the utter futility of this aging warhorse and after-hours rake, trying to get some grip on the winds of change in a pro ball culture he once knew so well. But look at it now! What was it? A runaway monster in the entertainment business, sucking up millions of dollars daily and engulfing the television screens, almost comic in its hypnotic hold on the sporting public. Societies of nuns went to pro football games. So did caravans of tourists from Japan. And why was Paul Hornung feeling futile?

He didn't know how pro football was ever going to regain its fundamental character of another time. Somebody on the show actually called it "soul."

Maybe we ought to stop right there. Are we serious about pro football with a soul? We're talking about a game played today by 300-pound tycoons wearing gold earrings, by acrobatic prodigies who can mug a defensive back at the height of their leap, grab the ball with one hand and come down with both feet in bounds. It is a game whose players in one recent year included one accused of trying to murder the mother of his unborn child. A second player, one of the game's best linebackers, was accused of murder a few weeks later. Another, drafted on the first round by the Vikings, tried to cut his throat in the despair of emotional problems. It's a game in which the hooliganism on the field (loony celebrations, helmet-to-helmet mayhem) matches some of the arrests for solicitation and drug use off the field.

Can this kind of game harbor a soul under the sweat and blood and casual crudity and mounting concussions? To this add immature college dropouts who become millionaires before playing a down in the NFL?

For some players, it can and does have a soul. Hornung didn't use the word, but it's probably what he meant when he said "camaraderie," which is a safer word for an ex-stud to use when he's talking about feelings on TV. Thank God he avoided "chemistry." Hornung acknowledged that today's ballplayers, for all of their wealth, are still capable of experiencing that peculiar bond that welds the electricity of a shared mission with their shared physical strength. It may come when they are in the midst of a two-minute drive to the goal line in a big game, or with the approach of a first Super Bowl. But Hornung seemed to think that in his day that feeling went deeper. It was the emotional contract of grown men playing a kid's game in dead earnest year after year, understanding the others' quirks and goofball flights, appreciating one another's refusal to yield to pain.

And when their careers were finished, they would remember those years and the respect that grew among them and never waned with time. Hornung sounded wistful. Today's game was still good, still exciting. Obviously. The ratings were off the charts. The public couldn't get enough. The athletes were as good or better than ever. If you played pro football today, and you were good at it, maybe only good enough to perform one special act well, you could get rich. You could get there if you did no more than center the ball accurately for punts and field goals.

And yet—

The old system might have been lousy and tyrannical in forcing ball players to work for the same owners until they got too old or slow to make the team. But the old system did make them a team. And maybe in the long run, that was better than the big money.

The camera was kind to Paul Hornung. The butter color hair of his hell-raising days had bleached with his approaching dotage, but it was still impeccably swept back in a meringue of white waves. No doubt about it, this guy was still a star and the camera seemed to acknowledge it with some accent lighting on the Golden Boy's profile—and the puzzlement in his eyes. He'd been impaneled as one of the elders of pro football to give the ballplayer's' evaluation of the state of the industry at the turn of the millennium. It was good and thoughtful television, especially by today's standards. The Golden Boy tried hard not to come across as an old crock crusading for the restoration of a time now vanished. Yeah, money has turned the game's stars into pricey jocks for rent. What are you going to do? Tell them not to take the money?

But Horning, the pragmatist, couldn't say what he wanted to say. He conceded that the game might be faster, the athletes today bigger and stronger, the techniques better. The offenses were more sophisticated and the defenses smarter. And pro ball had never been more popular. But somehow it was better forty years ago.

Not that the game was necessarily better then. So what was better? Hornung seemed to blink. It all looked surreal. What were they talking about here? Ball players make $5, $6 $10 million a year now, but it isn't enough. It isn't, because somebody is going to offer more. So what was better forty years ago, if the money was tame and paltry then and the game may not have been as good. Hurnung sighed and blinked again. Maybe it was the times, the old circle-the-wagons mentality of guys who had played together for years and who not only knew how to cover for a lineman who was playing on one good leg, but did it on every play.

I got up and began searching through some old files in my cabinets to retrieve a copy of a piece I wrote for the NFL's *Game Day* magazine in 1986. It was one of those stories that

John Wiebusch of *Game Day* wanted in the magazine every three or four years, about the growing legend of (who else?) Vince Lombardi. I called Hornung in Louisville. As we talked, we each inevitably drew a mental picture of the coach Hornung always called The Old Man—Lombardi with the archetypical southern Italian face, a broad pug nose and dark, inquisitive eyes that harbored something smoldering, almost glowing, inside them. I told Horning that if Hollywood had cast *The Godfather* in the 1960s, Lombardi would have beaten out Marlon Brando for the title role. Hornung laughed raucously. I said if they would have given Lombardi two months with the script, he would have outacted Brando. He laughed harder. It wasn't because the line was funny. He laughed because he thought it was true.

Every few years, sometime around the Super Bowl, when the audiences are the biggest, the networks rewind the Vince

Lombardi saga, and somehow it always seems worth it. Why? In a business filled with transitory heroes, Lombardi remains the idealization both of a game and a creed—of consuming, irreversible commitment.

"Tell me about Lombardi and those years of pro ball," I said to Hornung.

"He really talked the way you see it on those plaques," Paul Hornung said. "'Winning isn't everything, it's the only thing.' I don't care if he didn't invent that slogan. It was more Lombardi than whoever said it first. He said those things in our squad meetings and in the locker room. But he didn't do it with just words. There was nothing magic about his language. It was the way he dominated every room he walked into and everything he did. He was obsessed with doing it right, which means winning. A lot of coaches are. This guy knew how to win. He did it every place and in every weather. He got into your skin. For most of the guys who played for him, he somehow became the most important person in the world. He screamed and he threatened you and intimidated you. A few guys hated him for that. But they would have died rather than not play for him. They needed his approval. His personality was that powerful.

"You know, some guys, after they die, get bigger. The stories about them, especially if they were super successful people, inflate their personalities and what they did. It's not that way with Lombardi. He was big *then*. For ten years he was pro football in America, and he deserved that image. He walked into a small city in Wisconsin and took a bunch of guys going nowhere and turned them into one of the greatest football teams ever put together. It's not only that he did it, but the way he did it. He had values and ethics that went right to the core of what it takes and what it means to be a successful human being as well as a successful athlete. Yeah, he ranted and insulted. But when he talked about love on a football team—before everybody else did it and it got to be a cliché— he found a way to make that understood and believable. He wasn't talking about hugging. That was not exactly a huge thing in his life. He was talking about the sacrifices you had to make for each other, and about what the other player was going through when he was in pain or in some struggle.

"Everybody who played for him was forever changed by him in some way, and changed for the good, even if they didn't care for him. How many people can you say that about?"

For most of us, it's a short list. Maybe some of the saints are on it. But Lombardi certainly wasn't a saint. Ego? Yes, of course. Hornung cherishes his private encounters with Lombardi both when he played and in later years when Lombardi had moved on to Washington, D.C.

"I remember walking into a Washington restaurant with him. He got a standing ovation from the diners. It was a big and fancy restaurant and they all stood up. And when we got to our table, he couldn't resist. He had ego enough to appreciate all that. He said, 'Paul, how do you like it? This town is full of some of the biggest politicians in the world, and nobody notices. But the football coach walks in, and everybody applauds.'"

But they don't applaud every football coach. Lombardi knew that. He didn't have to say it. So what Hornung seemed to be lamenting on that TV show, far more than the game's takeover by the money god, was the erosion of the game's brotherhood. When free agency came and the salaries started soaring, the football hierarchs had to put in some kind of meaningful salary cap to survive their own spasms of covetousness—wanting to win so badly they could bankrupt the team in bidding wars. The best teams now couldn't hold onto all of their stars or even to some of the role players. They had to limit the number of tycoons they could afford. And often the fallout of that arrangement was a ruinous rivalry among some of the star position players on the team. If your status depended on the number of passes you caught, so did your earning power. And if you didn't catch enough passes to maintain your status, you were going to grumble. The quarterback was the fall guy, or the offensive coordinator, or the other guys who caught passes. It happens all the time in a pro football society of today where cash is king. And there goes the brotherhood.

And why was I smiling, this old crock of the newspaper city room, while Paul Hornung was lamenting? I was smiling because Hornung and I were on the same page. The pro football Hornung knew was the pro football I knew. I didn't know the inside game the way Hornung knew it, but I knew the players and the times. I knew the wackiness of it and the random savagery of it, the mediocre grunts who were usually the stars of the locker room brawls because the stars were smart enough to get out of there before the blood flowed. Was there really a special kind of brotherhood then as Hornung seemed to be suggesting? Yes, although it wasn't especially noticeable if the team went 0-for September and October. And were there "characters" then? True characters and not necessarily the loudmouth characters of the Shannon Sharpe schticks?

Lord, there were characters. So maybe for a while we can shut down all the dot coms on the Internet, and shut off Jaws Jaworski. (On what cable is Jaws tonight? How can you remember them all?) And we can revert ourselves to the early 1960s, when pro football was still a game and not a billion dollar sideshow and soap opera.

Walter Payton Dies, and Beautifies a Brutal Game

(written for Game Day *of NFL Publications, January 2000)*

Pro football is big and boisterous and often brutal. It is also glamorous and rich and overblown and sometimes heroic. There are times when it is so big and visible it is simply engulfing and comes very close to the preposterous.

Pro football has earned all of those characterizations and more. One thing it is rarely called is beautiful. But for one brief and unforgettable moment, in the aftermath of the death of Walter Payton, it shed its bombastic image and became beautiful.

And why was that? The language doesn't seem to fit. The game is about spectacle and the clash of powerful and driven men colliding with other powerful and driven men. Absorbing as that is, how are you going to extract beauty out of all that violence on the field, out of the vulgarity of the show business around it?

But you can. Years ago the Chicago football writers presented a plaque to a visiting player in the final seasons of his career. "Wouldn't football be a beautiful game," the inscription read, "if everyone played it the way Hugh McElhenny does?" McElhenny was almost the last of a culture—an open-field runner of nimble movement and style. He was a matador gliding through a herd of bulls. And there was beauty in the pure craft and art of a Joe Montana leading his team down the field against Cincinnati in the last crucial minutes of a Super Bowl, so flawlessly that in retrospect the outcome seemed inevitable.

What happened in the hours following the death of Walter Payton, though, transcended those other moments that you could honestly treasure. The hours after Walter Payton died created for professional football—its players, coaches and its followers—a solidarity of grief and affection that seemed to wash away every conflict that divided them. It did that for only one night, perhaps, but it was a night to cherish.

Payton was a marvelous football player, and also a human being of decency and honor, though he was also known for his streaks of good-natured intramural mischief. He was greeted with such unanimous fondness by his peers that they called him "Sweetness," both during his days on the field and after he retired. But in the hours after he died on November 2, 1999, Walter Payton, did for football what his football greatness and all of his records could not have done; what perhaps no other football player could have done. In remembering who and what he was, pro football came together in a way that was spontaneous, passionate and real. It cut across the entire range of fans and participants, bringing together the men who had played with him and against him, the coaches, younger players who knew him only through TV flashbacks, and fans who'd never seen him but trusted what the players said about him.

In those hours of mourning and celebration, pro football became a community again. The word has been horribly misused and twisted in America society, but this was an honest-to-God community. These were the faces of pro football speaking from a hundred TV studios and the multitudes of football watchers in front of their screens, bound in a remembrance of an extraordinary athlete and a good man.

Communities don't have to last to the end of time. Sometimes they are united for only a few hours, a few days. This one will last in the shared affection of that day. There will be other heroes like Walter Payton. But probably no one quite like Walter Payton.

What was different?

Here was a football player whose death could reach a harsh and willful man like Mike Ditka and others like him, and touch them with humility

It could reach stoical and undemonstrative football men like Bud Grant and others, and touch them with tenderness.

It could reach an uncompromising competitor like Mike Singletary, and touch him with peace.

No one who rode with him in a car or was victimized by some of his loony locker-room pranks is going to call Walter Payton a saint. But what his peers saw in Walter Payton the day of his death, and what they tried to express, came down to this: When you look at Payton as an athlete and as a life, he was about the best this game is going to be. He made other players proud to share the fraternity of pro football with him. They could see his commitment on every play and in every game and in every side of his life. Whether they were grouped in the huddle with him or lining up against with him across the scrimmage line, it made them better. Gabbing in a café with him after a game made the world a little lighter. Watching him struggle with his uncoming death, hearing him say without melodrama and with total conviction that he would not give in, made them grateful to know him. It made them believe there was an instinctive grace in how he played and lived. They will tell you that.

I wrote pro football in Minneapolis for a number of years. Although TV already had begun to transform pro football into a tasteless and unbridled extravaganza, it was nothing like today's Inside-the-NFL, with four talking heads, six nights of the week, followed by a three-hour pre-game show on Sunday, with Terry Bradshaw and Howie Long coming at you from every direction of the compass.

One chilly afternoon in 1975 Walter Payton came to Metropolitan Stadium just north of the cornfields in Bloomington. He was a rookie then. The Vikings' defense more or less suffocated everything in sight in those years. It had Alan Page, Jim Marshall, Carl Eller, Jeff Siemon, Wally Hilgenberg, Paul Krause and all their familiar accomplices. The team had squared off against the Pittsburgh Steelers in the Super Bowl the previous winter. Most of the fans had never heard of the Bears' Walter Payton.

Almost from the beginning of that game, Walter tore into and around the Viking dreadnoughts. He piled up the yards and he had the bratwurst-munching Met Stadium regulars in the full flight of jitters. He brought the Bears to the edge of winning—and then the rookie running back went to the sidelines for practically the whole fourth quarter.

Nobody knew why. In those years there were no chic young woman patrolling the sidelines with their microphones and their fur scarves and Fifth Avenue coiffeurs, eavesdropping on the coaches. So we were defenseless against the aggressive silence of the Bears' bench. The assumption was that Walter had pulled a muscle, something like that. He hadn't. Payton played the game so hard, fought the Viking all-pros with an outpouring of energy so relentless that he was hyperventilating. He could barely breathe. It would happen to him often in the next few years. At the time, it scared the Bears as much as it relieved the Vikings. When the game was over, Grant looked a little shaken, a condition rarely associated with Old Ironeyes. "The young guy," he told the reporters after the game, "is going to be some football player. He already is."

Shift to Soldier Field just two years later. By that time Payton had already reached some form of zenith as a football player. Playing once more against a Viking team that had appeared in yet another Super Bowl the previous January, Walter starting ripping up yardage immediately. By that time a seasoned veteran, he had brought to a fine art the distinctive stiff-legged kick that was his trade-mark as a running back. That kick would help propel him to an eventual 16,716 yards from scrimmage—more than anyone in the NFL had amassed before. When I first saw Payton's "kick" I dismissed it as a nifty and pardonable piece of showmanship.

There may have been a swatch of that. Who knows? But the more I learned about Payton by actually watching him play, the more convinced I became that this outflung leg was Walter's personal, impulsive gymnastics, intended not for more attention, but for more yardage. Payton did get attention that murky afternoon in Chicago. He didn't get much resistance. When they finished the arithmetic, it came to 275 yards.

In the Bears' locker room after the game (which they won 10-7), you could learn more about Walter Payton. The Bears swarmed him in their grimy arms and with their guttural chants and salutes. The idea of grown, muscular athletes loving each other sometimes gets sticky when the culture of the game is explored, but there was nothing superficial about it that day in the Bears' locker room. They ganged Walter Payton because he was *their* Walter, and he was one of a kind. He blocked with the same fury and purpose with which he ran. When a blitzing linebacker lined up the Bears' quarterback for decapitation, Walter got in the way. He didn't always put the blitzer on the ground, but he did stop him. No quarterback's head rolled when Walter blocked.

Not so oddly, the men who played against Walter Payton felt something very close to the same kind of kinship with him as the Bears' player who shared the huddle with him. They were rivals, but hardly enemies. Opposing players often and very candidly feel distaste or contempt for people on the other side because competition does that to competitive athletes. And, not so incidentally, those attitudes are easily fueled by a blindside block or a fist in the groin under the pile.

Nobody did that to Payton. He played the game the way it was written. From his earliest days in the league, he was seen as a player who delivered at the max every moment he was on the field, but as a human being and personality it was clear that he was going to be approachable and a good guy in any element.

He was the ball player every ball player want to be. And when he was dying, he didn't run from it. He fought it, but he admitted he was scared. He never lived nor played by empty slogans. Yet when he was at his best, the men who tried to stop him were convinced he could practically go on forever.

Forever ended on November 2, 1999.

I have always looked on the language of football players

as some of the most descriptive there is. I don't mean the TV-speak and the trash talk that the rhetoric often becomes. There was one term that got to be a little archaic because it tended to be confused with another use of the word. But when a football man sees another football man hurling every last grain of energy and commitment into a play, oblivious of risk, he will watch with respect and say, "There's a guy who sold out. Gave everything he had inside of him."

It was the way Walter Payton played football and also the way he lived. It is the way he will be remembered, with sweetness.

Carl Eller Finds His Grail

February 2004

The culture now allows grown men to cry at times that are not connected with funerals and IRS audits. I'm not sure I cried Sunday with the news of Carl Eller's election to pro football's Hall of Fame. But my glasses fogged, slowly but stubbornly.

I was in the kitchen when I heard the news. Just above the kitchen table there is a small painting of the monastery of Thyangboche in the Himalayas. I was looking around for something to high-five, and the painting had just the right height. The scene in the painting might have come out of Mother Goose, resembling an ancient castle in the snow. My hand touched it and I said "Way to go, Moose." Outside the window at 7 a.m. the snow floated through neighborhood evergreens, and, because this was a moment that deserved a celebration, the falling snow obliged. It became a shower of confetti greeting Carl Eller's arrival in the Hall of Fame on a winter's day.

I remembered Carl Eller struggling in the snow on Mt. Rainier in Washington. He wanted to climb a mountain, and I had experience in that kind of action. He asked me if we could be partners on the rope some day and I said, "Let's climb Rainier." He was in his last year of pro football, living and playing in Seattle, aging on the athletic calendar yet still strong as a Roman arch. But he wasn't a mountain man and he wasn't going to reach the summit. "You can get to Camp Muir a few thousand feet below the top, Moose," I said. "It's as good as a sack." He did and we high-fived in the twilight at 10,000 feet. Howling in triumph, he chugged and romped around in circles in the snow, making huge trenches in it with his Size 15 boots and 260-pound body. He was, in fact, big enough to start an avalanche. I slowed the celebration by pretending to tackle him and he scooped me up in all of my climbing gear, clamped me in a hug and shouted, "We're brothers."

We were. And I remembered another time when he'd used language like that, to his quarterback. The Vikings had come charging in from the snow and cold of their Toonerville old arena, Metropolitan Stadium, after winning the conference championship by beating the Los Angeles Rams on their way to their first Super Bowl. The dressing room was a circus of half-naked bodies hugging and dancing in the spreading delirium, their uniforms and skin caked with frozen grass and mud. Strips of adhesive tape littered the floor and disorganized voices sang wall to wall. Players thrust bottles of champagne in the air, saluting each other. Joe Kapp held one of the bottles. Joe was a longshoreman of a quarterback, a Hispanic from California. His jaw had been gashed by a broken beer bottle in a bar fight years earlier during his stint in Canada. It still bore the prints of forty-six stitches. When he threw the football his passes fluttered and lurched, and by temperament he should have been a linebacker or a night club bouncer. But the players loved him and none more than Carl Eller. Kapp and Eller had a special affinity, a kind of kinship forged by the struggles of their childhood, Kapp's on the West Coast, Eller's in the South.

And now, in the midst of the dressing room uproar, the powerful African-American from South Carolina spotted the roughneck Mexican-American from the shanties of California and rushed across the room to embrace him, waving his champagne. "Joe," he said, "you're my brother. You and me. We're the same."

Of all the memories I carried from the years when I wrote football, that scene is the engraving of what was right about the pro game if all of the sideshows and money glut of it were removed. This was a portrait of the athletic ideal in pro football. They DO sacrifice. Not all of them. The self-indulgence available to bigtime athletes today overwhelms some of them. But the one permanent reality for Eller and Kapp on that day wasn't the television or the frenzy or even the money, but the trust they placed in each other.

A hard-knuckled, sweaty love CAN grow up among some of them, and it is never more vivid than on a frozen field when the reliance that one man places in the man squatting and grunting beside him on the line of scrimmage is utter and complete.

That might now be expressed in the past tense. The money today is enormous. So is the visibility. But it might have been a comforting coincidence that a guy like Carl Eller was elected to the Hall of Fame on a weekend when the Super Bowl gave us one more glimpse of football from that older time when the brotherhood of the battle seemed more credible than it does today.

This was a football player, Eller, with his flaws and vulner-abilities written almost as large as his strength and the random ferocities of his play. There were Sundays when he did not bring all of his strength and will to the game. In later playing years he went broke spending hundreds of thousands of dollars to nurse a drug habit. Yet with his playing career over and his personal and business life in shreds, he turned himself around, humbled himself with his admissions of wasted years and the injury he had caused those in his life, and he became a mentor and advocate of sobriety. Recognizing that he was headed for destruction unless he found help, he saved himself.

When we met during this time of redirection in his life, I was stunned by the change. He had gone into a fledgling business that had begun to prosper. He wore a dark business suit and the look of a man entering a new world, cleansed by a full disclosure of the old one. Sometimes we shared a speaking platform during those years. His transformation, frail at the beginning, became real and inspiring later.

We were never close friends when he played in Minnesota and shouldn't have been, given the hazards for the reader of that kind of relationship. In the best years of his football career, I can't remember a player who so resembled an absolute force of nature. His size, 6-foot-5 and 260 pounds, would not make him conspicuous today. But in those years, the 1960s and '70s, he gave the appearance of a huge, helmeted Neanderthal, menacing and relentless, an image that might have concealed his basic intelligence and instincts for the game he played.

He would knock down passes, block kicks, recover fumbles and make open-field tackles with a style of sudden violence that took on the aura of scriptural vengeance. He looked ungainly when he ran crossfield with the flow of the play, but he ran with deceptive speed. With the Vikings' defense of those years, he had graduated from the days when he was a leisurely, irresponsible boy-giant to assume a place of leadership. He had the equipment for it, the size, the commitment and a big, throaty baritone voice that was enough to make laggards quail. One day in December it did.

Eller's biggest admirer on the Vikings of those years was Francis Tarkenton, the brainy and saucy quarterback who preceded Eller into the Hall of Fame years ago, along with Alan Page, coach Bud Grant, Ron Yary, and Paul Krause. In one of their playoff games the team was groping in disarray and came in at halftime full of doubt and unfocused. Eller grabbed the coaches' blackboard, flung it to the floor, and vowed, cursing, that if the game ended that way every man on the team was going to answer to Carl Eller.

Tarkenton confided the scene later. The players had a nickname for the beat writer in those days. "Klobey," Francis said, "I want to tell you about Eller when we came in. He made this scene. The blackboard went smash. He was bellowing. His eyes were blazing. He looked like the giant on a rampage. When he looked into our faces, roaring about getting our asses in gear or else, I wanted to disappear. I was ready to jump into my locker to get out of the way." Instead, he took a more practical route. Francis and the others got all of the requisite body parts in gear and won the game in the second half.

Prime time athletes today rarely lack for some form of adoration, of attention or boxcar salaries. Gold championship rings set some of them apart as the elite in their trade. Athletes lust for those prizes. But gold rings don't match the ultimate mark of recognition, which is the Hall of Fame of their fraternity.

So Eller has reached that ultimate prize, after all of the convolutions of his life. He earned it during those years of congealed blood on his face in the muck of the old stadium. Oblivion followed, and then the discovery of another and better Carl Eller.

It was a just reward, a true summit.

The Olympics—Good, Bad and Glorious

February 2002

(Special to the *Christian Science Monitor*)

Salt Lake City—Two cross-country skiers, running on their last reserves, stopped abruptly on the top of a slope, side by side, a few hundred yards from the finish line. They glared at each other, a Norwegian and an Italian, each silently taunting the other to start first.

It was a game of tactical chicken, scornfully waged, each seeking the favored position of skiing second into the sprint. Finally the Norwegian led off, flinging a snarl at his rival as he did. They traded the lead twice, almost falling from exhaustion. The Norwegian won, and the Italian banged his ski pole in disgust.

It wasn't one of those scenes of overcooked emotion the cameras so love. But it was naked combat at the highest level of athletic competition, and it will be a portrait I'll carry away from the Winter Olympics of 2002 long after the hurrahs and howls of distress have subsided.

Let me confide that although I wrote about these Olympics as a newsman, I saw them fundamentally as you would—as a spectator, fascinated, inquisitive, and ready to be amazed.

To make sense of the scene here, you have to accept the world as a place where good folks coexist with rogues and thieves. You have to accept that on any given day, life will nourish both dreams and ideals, but it is also likely to be grossly unfair, cruel, wacky and simply baffling. It is full of both beauty and chaos. If you have made peace with that kind of world, you cannot help being lit up by the Winter Olympics, where the heroics contend daily with the finger-pointing hypocrisies. Much of the heroism is staggering, unadulterated athleticism, but some of it is won by the popular vote of judges who are as likely to sustain an "ours vs. theirs" attitude as they are to be honest and scrupulous.

Salt Lake 2002 gave you the whole montage. It spun the glorious with the ludicrous. The first and irreversible truth about the Olympics is that they imitate the real world. All of the reformers on earth aren't going to change that. There was enough paranoia from the Russians and others and enough piety and political muscle from the North American side to fill the quotas.

On the other hand, you had to have a heart of brick if the Olympics did not leave you tingling at the sight of athletes drained but transfixed by what they had achieved, standing on a podium in tears at the sound of their homeland hymns. The Olympics turned you speechless at the bravura of a Janica Kostelic. She charged through the slalom gates, smiling in exhilaration at being alive in this tick of time on her way to a third gold medal for Croatia. You were agape at the leaping incandescence of Sarah Hughes and then her teenage yelps.

But Salt Lake also left you with rolling eyes and a wobbly psyche in the day-after-day crises provoked by the same forces—nationalism, the smugness of power, suspicion and envy—that cause nastier conflict and more lethal results in the real world. If you could handle all that with some sense of entertainment, it meant this: you could leave the games having achieved enough emotional balance to applaud the beautiful and transcendent without being turned into a grumbling curmudgeon by the bizarre and hysterical.

I shared America's elation at its athletes' remarkable run on medals from end to end, felt it without being especially surprised. Why would one be surprised? We had the money, we had the home field, we had the incentive and the crowds and, of course, we had the marvelous athletes. I stared at those aerialists-from-Mars who spun and somersaulted and laughed themselves silly, and I wondered how the human body could be capable of such contortions while suspended from skies and boards and forced to grapple with the humorless demands of gravity. I was stirred by young men and women, some of them wealthy, some of them ski bums, risking it all, bombing the slopes and ice sheets with fundamentally only one fear—that they might not deliver all that was in them.

And yet for all of those spectacles and the fire we saw in the eyes of those who so desperately needed to win, what moved me most about the Olympics was the mingling of faces and tongues of the world. You don't have to be a romantic to feel that. For two weeks this was Main Street, Earth. Almost. I add a qualifier, because kids don't grow up playing on snow and ice in Egypt and Indonesia. Throwing out the bureaucratic haggling, it was a global party in which no blows were landed or embassies burned, and for this the security armies could take a bow. I went for walks through the arenas and the avenues to banter with the Scandinavians and Russians, and I was nearly blown away by a slaphappy Dutch brass combo in front of the E Center. I was not approached by the Mormons as a candidate for conversion , but I was mistaken once for a Uzbeki. If the people of the world intrigue you, this was a Mother Lode. The townspeople were obsessed with offering hospitality. The security was restrained and competent.

There was a hidden tab for all of this. The American public shouldn't be gullible about it in the euphoria over their medals. Millions of dollars in taxpayer money will ultimately spin off to benefit people who did not compete for medals. Snow Basin, the scene of the alpine races, profited from a congressional grant of 1,377 prime acres of National Forest Land—the public's land—in exchange for 11,575 acres someplace else in the county.

That, of course, is the current wave of Olympics. The money is so vast now—TV rights, sponsorships, endorsements—that they will be forevermore the Corporate Olympics. But there is one added windfall for an immigrant culture like America's, now grown so rich and dominant, trying to govern the world.

Our immigrant blood here was the same blood that flowed in the veins of those skiers from Norway and the jumpers from the Balkans. And for a brief space of time we were together. A man of the second generation of his immigrant Slovenian family—mine—could stand and watch the Slovenian ski jumpers struggling for a solitary medal. Their faces evoked the faces of underground iron miners with whom my father worked in northern Minnesota so many years ago. I recognized the names and faces of Slovenian skiers. They were mine. And when the team's last man jumped and landed and Slovenia won its one medal, I high-fived the woman next to me and said "*Dobro*. Good show." And so it was.

The Carry-Out Boy Wins Gold

February 2002

(Special to the *Christian Science Monitor*)

S **alt Lake City** — He flattened his body between his v-shaped
skis until he was flying almost at the horizontal. The sight
was unearthly. His arms were pinned back to his sides and he
sailed and sailed through the western ski liked some helmeted
Superman, his nose between his ski tips until —

Superman finally plunked to earth and stood revealed, to
all appearances, as the carryout boy from the corner Safeway.

That is not exactly how Simon Amman is carried on the
official dossiers of the 2002 Winter Olympics. But it is how his
face and his adolescent exuberance are going to be remembered
by the enthralled thousands who stood on the rims of the ski
jumping landing zone and by the television millions.

What they'll remember is not so much his unheralded
dual gold medals in the 90K and again in Wednesday's 120K
ski jumping. What they're not likely to forget is the pure and
unguarded astonishment in the eyes and yelping voice of a 20-
year-old Swiss mountain kid discovering that he was, gulp, an
Olympic champion.

What was it like, Simon?

"It felt so GOOD! I knew right away after takeoff that this
was the jump. I was trembling. There are no words for this. I
was so nervous. After takeoff I was flying away. It has been a
crazy day. A crazy week. I never would have believed I could
be the champion. In the air, and now, it is such a good, such a
GREAT feeling."

And how far, Simon?

Well, you don't do the conversions floating above the
snow, trying to keep your body inert yet straining for a few
more meters, a few more inches, and trying to look pretty all

of the time for the style points. The computers recorded the distance on that jump at 133 meters, which means well over 430 feet.

Was this something out of Mother Goose and Aesop's Fables, Simon? It was close to that because here was a yodeling kid from the Alps who came back out of nowhere, the wreckage of a crash landing last month. And when they did all of the tabulations he was ahead of the great jumpers, Adam Malysz of Poland and Sven Hannawald of Germany and Matti Hautamaeki of Finland. And now, for the rest of his life they are going to call him what suddenly became the catchiest *nom de plume* of the Olympics: "Swiss Air."

Clearly, there are more heroic figures than Simon Amman in this quadrennial feast of speed and reckless quest mixed in with the usual intrigue of suspected skullduggery in figure skating. But if you missed all the rest and saw only the kid from Switzerland soaring into the Olympic history books, and then blinking and flapping his arms to convince himself that it was real, you saw enough to make the 2002 Olympics indelible.

Sometimes it's good to remind ourselves that these are not, after all, super men and women. They are human beings of remarkable skills and strength but frailer than most emotionally—because of their huge commitment of ego and ambition, and because the competition at their level of performance is so relentless. When you're tempted to forget that, a Simon Amman emerges to restore the Olympics, just momentarily, to the innocence and the ideal they lost somewhere between the olive groves of ancient Greece and the billion dollar budgets of today.

A Hard Man to Love on Sunday Afternoon

August 2000

(Most of the younger football wonks I meet today will hear the name of Norm Van Brocklin and place him somewhere between Socrates and Abner Doubleday. They will then remember that he's got something to do with old time ball games and, probably, professional football. I make a game effort to tell them that the times weren't that ancient, and that the Dutchman truly was the man who made Sunday afternoon football the first guts-and-all virtual reality survival show in American entertainment.)

The only sound that gave Van Brocklin any peace on Monday mornings after his Minnesota Viking misfits lost a football game was the voice of Ray Charles, singing his torch ballads that made millions of folks misty in the '60s.

The only places within driving range of Ray Charles on Monday mornings were the jukeboxes of the blue collar 3.2 beer joints on Lake Street in Minneapolis. Van Brocklin would telephone me around 10 o'clock in the morning.

He rarely introduced himself. "You still writing about that lousy football game?" he asked.

"It's Monday morning," I said. "It's already in the paper."

"Yeah, I read it. Every golden syllable. How the hell do you make a turkey like that sound like a football game? I'm ashamed of the way we played."

"The readers already know that," I said. "You said it on three different pages in the newspaper. I thought your team was respectable, coach. You play Green Bay and lose by only three touchdowns. They're better than you at every position.

I don't know how you could have played them much better. Lombardi said as much after the game."

Norm Van Brocklin almost gagged. "The goddamned spaghetti eater. He had us by the nuts and he knew it. I couldn't believe how he sucked us in on that play pass. Did you see it?"

This was standard Monday morning dialogue between the coach and the journalist in the 1960s. Van Brocklin didn't want to replay the game. He wasn't looking for reinforcement. He want-ed to exorcise something that boiled inside him after each loss. What he wanted was to get out of the house or the office or wherever he spent Monday mornings and listen to Ray Charles.

I said I was at the stadium Sunday and managed to notice the play he brought up. It was basic football. Bart Starr faked a handoff to Jim Taylor into the line. The Vikings mobbed Taylor. Starr turned, still holding the ball and threw fifty yards downfield to Boyd Dowler. It's called a play action pass. Eventually even the best defensive backs get burned by it.

"Dowler is just standing, waiting for the football to come down," Van Brocklin groaned, "and our guy [Rich Mostardi, the safety] is still looking into the backfield twenty yards away. He has no idea where the ball is or where Dowler is."

I could imagine the royal chewing-out facing Mostardi when they did the films. I thought somebody ought to lobby for him. "It was a good fake by Starr," I said. "I was fooled myself."

The Dutchman's mood suddenly changed. He sounded delighted to hear the news, his suspicions confirmed. "Oh, that's beautiful," he said. "That qualifies you to write pro football."

The Dutchman's snarls had receded. He was giggling over his punchlines. What he needed in these day-after sparring sessions was an excuse to be sociable again. He usually followed with a gruff invitation to listen to Ray Charles. We drove around, found a place and ordered Cokes. Van Brocklin got some quarters and fed the jukebox. Ray Charles started singing. "I Can't Stop Loving You." It was wistful and moody but, for Van Brocklin, oddly healing. I thought, here was the voice of a blind man coming out of a machine in a gloomy beer parlor in the middle of the morning. His sound and art were guileless, easy and personal. They seemed to spread some form of solace over this pathologically competitive man festering from the loss of a football game that was not exactly going to change the course of the world. The scene, I thought, was slightly comic: Ray Charles' therapy parlor at ten in the morning. The Dutchman took a few moments to drift into a reverie. "Isn't this guy great?" he asked. I nodded. How could anybody not respond to the songs of Ray Charles? To validate this opinion, Van Brocklin played "I Can't Stop Loving You" six times in the next hour. For a change of pace, he asked me what I liked from Ray Charles. I said "Try 'Georgia On My Mind.'" Van Brocklin played 'Georgia' six times.

Meanwhile, we talked football on and on. It was all off the record. The only other customers in the tavern were two guys wearing denim work jackets drinking beer at the bar. In the year 2000 on Monday morning they would be yammering about the Vikings game. But this was 1961. They talked for an hour about the weather. In another culture an eavesdropper would have been floored by this performance. It was non-stop gabbing about the weather, fixing the furnace, greasing the snow blowers, trading in the snowmobile for a new model next month, bitching about not getting off for the deer season, backtracking to the worst wind-chill in Minnesota last January. Why would the eavesdropper be surprised? This was Minnesota. Delirium over pro football and baseball did not come suddenly or naturally in Minnesota, where watching the ice form on Lake Minnetonka is still an important spectator sport. In 1991 three hours after the Twins beat Atlanta in the final game of the World Series, a fan honking his horn to celebrate was arrested in the suburbs for disturbing the peace.

If it were today the two barflies would recognize the Viking coach the minute he walked through the door. Two days later the town would be wired with rumors of the Minnesota Vikings head coach spending all Monday morning drinking beer in a bar. You could predict the aftermath. TV camera crews would stake out the tavern. The bartender would be an instant celebrity, interviewed for every news show in the Twin Cities plus Sports Center on ESPN and Fox. But this was 1961. Van Brocklin was the Vikings' first coach. The guys at the bar didn't recognize him. They would have ignored him if they did.

For most of my years of association with Van Brocklin, we got along with some rough version of mutual respect. It was also wariness. Still, we laughed a lot. Those attitudes were often interrupted by long sieges of mutual antagonism and once by a near fist fight in Detroit. A neutral would probably say we had the kind of combative personalities that were bound to collide. The long interludes of frigid silence that followed were usually more damaging to me than to Van Brocklin, because he was the one and only authority on the team. And if I didn't quote Van Brocklin during the week, somebody on the newspaper, then the *Minneapolis Tribune*, was certain to do it, leaving me to gnaw on my misguided sense of honor.

We had some romping good times in those honky tonks. I was never quite sure what motivated our sessions and I'm deadly certain that no managing editor would condone them today. Maybe it's what Van Brocklin needed to quell the rages inside him. He was a brainy guy in a violent business, to which he contributed more than his share of violence. When he was calmer and the talk got around to college football, he would confess, without boasting about it, that he needed only three years to earn a degree at the University of Oregon. But turmoil was at the core of his professional environment, and if the day was short on turmoil he managed to concoct some. Creative as he was with his strategies and impulses, as a football coach he was a horror show for any self-respecting psychologist. He was vile and abusive with his players, sardonic and just plain domineering. Off the field (usually) his ethnic slurs were proverbial. He talked privately about some of the African-American players, but not all, in language that today would be considered abominable, and was abominable then.

In this he was hardly alone. In his racism he was no better nor worse than most. On the field he was impartial enough. He would often rail against the lack of heroism (his view) of a black halfback. But he would do the same of a white quarterback. He was a football creature of his time and his culture. Words like "nigger" and "black asses" were a common part of the conversation currency in the coaching lingo of those years, which didn't make them any more forgivable. Some coaches didn't use them. Lombardi and Tom Landry didn't. Don Shula didn't. There were others. When Van Brocklin sometimes brought them into our conversations, I didn't deliver lectures. Piety doesn't usually wear well in the macho societies. Sometimes I just walked away. What I should have done was to write it before I eventually did. But those conversations *were* private. Under the rules of engagement they were handled as such by most if not all of the people in my business. If one is allowed retrospect, what would have stopped it quickly would have been the presence of black reporters on the scene. There were none. The newspaper personnel departments in those years weren't any more magnanimous in racial attitudes than the coaches. There are mounting numbers of African-American writers and coaches today, of course, and the racial issue—while still capable of erupting—is being resolved. If it weren't, the players themselves would have organized a revolution, since the overwhelming majority of quality players in America's major pro leagues are players of color. Looking backward, when you say the racial drift of many football coaches of thirty and forty years ago reflected the society of the time, it leaves you with only one available truth. God, the abuse we so casually inflicted on people.

As a coach Van Brocklin was no one-dimensional ogre, which we can talk about in a few minutes. But he coached in an attitude of constant wrath and was hounded by the suspicion that most of his football players were malingerers, unsalvageable mediocrities, or just plain dumb. He actually had more players of quality in his early years in Minnesota, and his later years in Atlanta, than he was willing to admit to himself. Fran Tarkenton was already a star in his rookie season, tough, clever and gifted. Van Brocklin's highest redeeming quality as a coach was an ability to lift players of limited skills to a playing level beyond those skills. He was a creature of will, impulse, intellect and ego. His greatest virtue as a competitor was his unbreakable belief in himself. When his ferocities could no longer push his younger players to levels they couldn't sustain, Van Brocklin became a certified tyrant, cruel and vindictive. He lost control of the players and ultimately raged himself out of football.

His tongue was tart, inventive and memorable. Nobody could puncture a bumbling football player with Van Brocklin's originality and his four-letter eloquence. In their first year the Vikings employed a field goal kicker, Mike Mercer, who was one of the nomads of his time in college and pro football. He attended four or five different colleges, with his kicking tee and resumes in hand. For a variety of reasons, his tenure at all of them was brief. He was a likeable enough guy but moved about with the wariness of a man worried about getting hit by a passing freight train. It didn't matter that there were no railroad tracks in sight. Field goal kickers tend to paranoia. Mercer usually wore a crew cut that gave him the appearance of a

German infantryman about to hit the trenches. He had a strong but erratic leg. He would kick field goals from 47 yards out but miss them from 20. He did this did not once but twice in a game at Metropolitan Stadium. The second time, sensing a torrent of vitriol from Van Brocklin, Mercer shunned the direct route to the bench and made a long loop around the cheerleaders in the hope that Van Brocklin was occupied with somebody else's bumblings. His strategy had no chance of working. Van Brocklin didn't wait for Mercer. He pursued him. He yanked off Mike's helmet and gave him a terse evaluation of his work.

"Mercer,' he screamed, "you couldn't kick a whore off a pisspot."

Mike heard this novel judgment in silence. If he laughed he would have been fired. If he applauded Van Brocklin's punchy rhetoric he would have been fired. If he argued he would have been fired. So he kept his mouth shut.

And, of course, he was fired.

You could look at this tumultuous personality, Van Brocklin's, and regret the absence of some grace and balance in it, something to make it more agreeable over the long haul. But that's a flip judgment, not quite fair. Van Brocklin sometimes brought his workaday tempests home with him, but he also brought a familial love that was constant. His wife, Gloria, was his partner, confessor and his champion. His daughters adored him, with reason. With them he was a generous and demonstrative man, as he was with two Asian youngsters he and his wife adopted in later years.

The professional relationships that developed between a reporter and the players and coaches he was covering, were fundamentally different in those days than they are today. In most of the cities, even the large metropolitan cities, one newspaper, one reporter, covered the team. Those relationships tended at times to be personal. Publishers in that era were either more forgiving or less aware of the potential for conflicts of interest. Today they insist on arm's length relationships between journalist and source, and they should. The culture of today's massive coverage really doesn't permit close contact off the field or out of the media room. But what it meant in the 1960s was that a solitary reporter, prowling the practice field daily, had a professional football team practically as a private preserve.

Once a week, maybe for 10 minutes or so on a Friday afternoon, a local TV station would show up with a camera. After the practices I'd kick field goals with a Jim Christopherson or Freddie Cox, or stand in the pass-catching line at the end of practice for one of Tarkenton's throws. It was that informal. A little nutty, when you think about it today. So one day Van Brocklin, sounding waggish and conspiratorial, told the other coaches he was going to find out if I knew anything about catching a football. The coaches usually called me "Barney." The title was bestowed by Van Brocklin. It was a throwback to the era of Barney Oldfield, the automobile racer. Van Brocklin thought I drove a car like a man inviting a wreck. "Barney," he said, "Go down five yards and run an arrow." The arrow was what most people call a slant pattern, in which the receiver goes down field a few yards and then cuts cross-field. Van Brocklin was not far removed from his championship years as an NFL quarterback. His arm was still one of the most powerful in football although he almost never displayed it in the Viking workouts, refusing to grandstand. But he thought this day might be a good one to come out of retirement. He told me how many strides to make before looking for the ball. I have to give him credit for that much chivalry. "On 3," he said. He barked the cadence. Hut. Hut. Hut. I came off the line in my wing-tip shoes and my polo shirt and broke cross-field. After the fifth stride I looked up, and the ball hit me in the gut. What it did, in fact, was to knock me on my duff. The ball hit so hard it all but rearranged my insides, but before it did, I pulled my arms around it. This was no athletic move. It was purely a self-preservative reflex. I went down and held on to the ball. The Dutchman's coaches applauded. They didn't applaud too loudly because they weren't sure Van Brocklin approved the scene all that much.

He did, though. The Dutchman's guffaws bounced off the seats of the homely little stadium. He came over. "You did well, " he said. "You can catch. You could play for this team if you had any brains."

I told him if I had any brains I'd give the job to somebody else.

The Dutchman died of a massive brain hemorrhage in the 1980s. The men he played with and against remain awed to this day by the ferocity, the unflinching will and the skills with which he played quarterback. Of his coaching years, they get philosophical. Some great players can make it as coaches; some can't. Some have the balanced personalities and patience to make it; some don't. Most of them consigned Van Brocklin to the second category, and the record seems to support that judgment. Neither in Minnesota nor Atlanta, though, was he actually evicted. From start to finish, in football, from the Los Angeles Rams to the Philadelphia Eagles, to coaching in Minnesota and Atlanta he pretty much decided when he was going to hit the road.

In a newspaperman's career, the days of Van Brocklin were too vivid to forget or, in fact, to rationalize or sanitize. I never completely figured out our Monday mornings with Ray Charles. Maybe he wanted to grind his axes by privately ripping the players he didn't like in ways that he wanted to avoid in his coaching meetings. He liked to confide some of his schemes for next Sunday. Maybe there was some therapy in it for him. He was also doing some fishing. He wanted to know what his players were saying about him in the locker room. He never put it that bluntly but that was the idea. I usually laughed off those little expeditions and told him if he wanted a mole he could get one at the zoo.

For ten years after his last season with the Vikings, we didn't exchange a word. Somebody told him about a remark I made about him, which was miles away from what I actually said, both in tone and substance. He called, screamed and shouted, and hung up. He didn't ask for an explanation, and I didn't think I had to give one. He coached at Atlanta for a few years, later did some TV analysis and adopted two Asian children. When he died in Georgia, Gloria asked me if I would be one of the speakers at his service outside their home south of Atlanta. In my little eulogy I said that for all of his storms in football, he was capable of kindness and a genuine humanity. When a family asked for a football for a sick kid, he'd bring the squad together and produce an autographed ball in five minutes. He offered money to old pros who were broke or drunk. He gave his roof and love to kids from halfway around the world, and when he finally left football he did it his way, snorting defiance and refusing to compromise. He came from a time when the coach was an autocrat. The players could be roustabouts and they might be hung over on Sunday but they sucked it up and played.

Van Brocklin was often wrong-headed and too often unfair. But he was real; he left a mark on the game he played and coached, and he was an original. I've missed our good times. And there are moments, driving Lake Street in Minneapolis, when I swear I can hear the breezy and forgiving voice of Ray Charles.

VI. The World Begins a New Millennium and the Road to Sanity Narrows

The Day a Skyscraper Melted Before Our Eyes

September 12, 2001

Minneapolis—We drove to a collection station for donated blood yesterday, Susan and I, three hours after the terrorist hijackers turned the World Trade Center towers into an inferno and the Pentagon into a mortuary.

The blood bank in Minneapolis, more than a thousand miles from New York and Washington, was jammed with American citizens, offering their blood to the victims of the horror playing out endlessly on the nation's television screens. The crowd of donors spilled into the parking lots, overwhelming the small staff of attendants. Men and women waited for three and four hours to give blood. A man with a clipboard took our names. He asked if we could return tomorrow. We said we would.

I closed my eyes before getting into the car. I don't mind confessing an emotion I couldn't have imagined under the conditions. I felt pride. My skin tingled. These were my neighbors. They were giving, instantly and unconditionally. They were saying to the people of New York, "We are together." Those words are not often spoken in America, a land of such vast diversity in its faces and language and culture, where some of the hostilities and racial fears of the old worlds are re-created here.

I live in the American heartland. Here, it is called the Midwest. Minneapolis the city and Minnesota the state have given the world some of its finest medicine, the technology of heart and kidney transplants and more. They have given America some of its greatest innovations in education, in the electronic industry, and in social justice. We have not always been generous in how we see the people of New York City. Here in the Midwest, we tell ourselves, we are calmer, more tolerant, less volatile with our opinions and language.

New Yorkers, we often think, are noisy and rude, defensive and judgmental.

But on our television screens, we saw the heart and soul of New York City in its agony and grief, a city where hundreds of firefighters and police went to their deaths trying to save those trapped in the collapsing towers.

We saw a New York City frightened and savagely torn, but exerting a humanity, a brotherhood we had not seen. The mayor of New York, a man hounded by personal turmoil and illness and ridiculed not so long ago, walked in the rubble and smoke clouds and gave voice to the city's stricken citizens. "We will overcome this," he said.

The people of Europe have witnessed similar sights—of leaders walking through war-devastated streets. They have seen this in Britain, Russia and dozens of other countries. But America had been spared those sights. We fought in wars. But usually they were somebody else's war or they were somewhere else.

And now America has been attacked, in its greatest cities, and now it is vulnerable. We saw that yesterday. Fanatics stole our airplanes in the sky and, slaughtering the American passengers in them, drove those planes into the landmarks of America, where thousands more were killed.

So for the first time in our history, the American war dead were strewn among the broken girders and melted glass of

America's once-elegant buildings, the symbolic gemstones of its power and wealth. And now New York lies wounded, but not broken. And what we, its neighbors in the Midwest, saw on our screens, was the spirit of a great city lifted and ennobled in its grief, its deaths and destruction, and in its resolve.

The city of Eastern bankers and pushing throngs, the mixed faces and tongues of the world, was transformed. This was the headstrong city so often noisy and impatient, proud of its Broadway and its Times Square and its lofty buildings and its arts, and never terribly well informed about the rest of America. This city, in its pain and torment and its bravery, became the heart of America.

photo Mike Zerby, *Star Tribune*/Mpls. St Paul

Wellstone Reminded Us
of the Nobility of an Ideal

February 2003

The Senate of the United States, accustomed to dealing with political heavyweights from the state of Minnesota, was not prepared for the arrival of a gnome.

But he didn't escape their notice. The old lion Republicans grunted in character, making no attempt to conceal their disapproval. Democrats sighed warily. The little guy talked a lot. He was spry and effervescent, hungry to learn. He tried too hard and too quickly to get acquainted, carrying around a tape recorder to preserve his early impressions. It was an act that seemed to make hash out of starchy standards of senatorial behavior.

The lions decided quickly that this was no Walter Mondale or Eugene McCarthy and, despite their mutual fondness for the spoken word, this definitely was no Hubert Humphrey.

Most of them slowly revised their judgment of Paul Wellstone in the years ahead. They saw a man growing in his knowledge of the institution, swift to understand both the limits and the (admittedly slim) opportunities of his idealism. But he never walked away from those ideals. The most sulphurous of the right wing ideologues came to find him an enjoyable and infectious personality and an energetic mind. Moreover, they found in this little warrior from the academic groves of Northfield, Minnesota, a spunk and commitment to the voiceless of America that never swerved and almost never compromised. They learned what his critics wouldn't, or couldn't, learn—that standing alone against the full roar of ninety-nine voices, which Wellstone occasionally did, was not a stunt or a transparent plunge into martyrdom.

"There's always a chance," he'd say, "that they were right and I was wrong." And then he'd mischievously wrinkle his forehead in a way that suggested there was legitimate doubt about that. "It could have been that I was the only guy in the room who had it right."

Loyalty to an idea was the grail of Wellstone's politics and his life. He lived to confront a truth that his colleagues understood full well, yet had learned to sidestep when the pressure got unduly heavy from the campaign contributors, or the president, or God knows who else. That truth was the vulnerability of average Americans to the bulldozers of power politics, wealth and greed. It was worse for the underclass—the poor, the ailing, and the silent and powerless of the minorities.

The day after he was killed in the crash of a light plane in northern Minnesota, a week before the election in which he was seeking another term, a newspaper woman on the East Coast telephoned. We'd worked together on newspaper pieces in the past. She wanted a few stories and impressions of Paul Wellstone. I said I hadn't covered him in the senate, but I knew him a little more than casually, had shared a couple of speaking platforms with him, admired him and was broken up by his death. I said I'd help but most of the anecdotes were available on the Internet.

She knew that but she still wanted to talk. She wanted to know what the Democrats would do to field a candidate against the Republican, Norm Coleman, but what neither of us suspected was the deepening anguish ahead for the Democrats. There would be a celebration of Paul Wellstone's life attended by thousands of his mourners, including Republican and Democratic colleagues from the Senate. In it one of Paul Wellstone's family friends would give a passionate, well-intentioned but terribly wrong speech that would alienate not only many in the building but thousands of Minnesota voters. And Coleman would defeat Walter Mondale, who volunteered to stand in for Paul Wellstone.

But that was days ahead and the East Coast reporter confessed knowing Wellstone only by the news stories and his reputation as an unsinkable populist who carried the banners and the bandages for the underdogs of American politics.

"Was that about right?" she asked.

I said it was essentially what Wellstone did in his political life. But how he did it, I thought, was just as fascinating.

"Tell me," she said.

"There were times when he really seemed to belong in a comic opera. He dressed eclectically, if you want to be kind. He'd arrive at a fund-raiser for a Democratic candidate, wearing a suit jacket that should have been in the dry cleaner's two days ago and a stained necktie in five colors hanging close to his knees. It could have been used as a tow rope. The crowd was instantly engaged. He'd pump his fist and make a joke about his ailing leg and apologize for taking speaking time away from the candidate, and he'd play it that way: the little guy who didn't want to get in the way of more profound speakers and more important business. And, of course, the candidate kept egging Wellstone to keep talking because the crowd was loving it, and sooner or later somebody was going to break out with a chorus of "Happy Days Are Here Again," the old and almost deceased rallying carol of the Democrats of FDR.

"That was Wellstone's heaven. He campaigned in a little green bus that looked ready for repossession. The tone of his campaign and his politics really wasn't 'us against them.' It was closer to 'there are more of us than you think.' He meant people who saw the America of his time, a country enormously wealthy, enormously strong, but still unable to break through the entrenchments of corporate power in America to lift up those who had been left behind. And most of those, he said, had been left behind not because they were lazy or irresponsible but simply because the alignment of politics and money in America froze them out.

"He died with the affection of scores of people in the Senate who thought he was a largely ineffectual politician. In this they may have been partly right. But they found themselves liking this little guy. Why? Because he reached out for their friendship, didn't betray that friendship, was a bright and delightful human being and, finally, understood the reality of America far better and more intimately than some of those who wielded the power.

"In the end, what they admired in him was a quality many of them had abandoned long ago: The willingness to fight the good fight, to cherish a cause and to argue it with intelligence and fervor to the end, against the current if he had to.

"The best thing he did, I thought, was to take time. He gave an angry voter or a frightened voter, or any voter, all the time he could spare. He would talk to media people for as long as they needed and to young political candidates with as much wisdom and inspiration available to him. He cared, and it didn't matter who needed his time, his energy or his comfort."

Months after the election I thought about the worst irony of his death in the northwoods of Minnesota. Of all the politicians I knew, this one was the most forgiving of human frailty. In the end it might have been human error—in the cockpit—that took his life. It's not stretch to guess that this, too, he would have forgiven.

Jesse the Body Had More
Craft Than Nero

February 2000

(Special to the *Christian Science Monitor*)

The music had ended. But the sounds of Zoltan Kocsis' bravura performance of Liszt's *First Piano Concerto* were still airborne as the audience pressed toward the exits of Minnesota's Orchestra Hall. That audience carried a retired Minneapolis newspaper columnist with it toward an unprogrammed encounter with an angry woman who wanted to unload her wrath.

She had no time for intramural talk about Kocsis and Liszt. The target of her furies on this night for longhair music lovers was a baldheaded politician named Jesse, a.k.a., The Body. This is Jesse Ventura, the talk show gadfly, the muscular Midas of politics, elaborately paid football analyst and, incidentally, the governor of Minnesota. This is a man of mind-bending, oddball portfolios that now include one that could only have done justice to a paranoid Roman Emperor. Jesse's latest is an attempted act of revenge against nosy reporters at the State Capitol. He wants each to wear a credential badge identifying himself or herself as an "Official Jackal."

"What are you going to do about Ventura?" the woman demanded.

I told her I'd rather talk about Liszt. I also told her that mothballed columnists have less clout than live ones. I did say that Ventura was probably an improvement on Nero. He's made more money being goofy and he hasn't yet threatened to throw newspaper reporters to the lions.

He is, though, only halfway through his four-year term.

There are a couple of truths about Ventura that may have escaped people around the country who've always pictured Minnesota as a haven for normalcy and admired it for its stolid acceptance of ten-foot snowbanks. These folks now want to know how Minnesotans could have elected a noisy cowboy to run their once-orderly homestead. The first surprise about Minnesota is that it is not predominately appalled by a pro wrestler governing the state, at least by this pro wrestler. The reason is that they don't expect normal behavior out of Ventura as a governor. They do expect normal governors to avoid using the public office in a candid grab for outside money because of its visibility and whatever power it has.

Ventura candidly grabs for outside money.

His take so far must run toward a million dollars, culminating in his current role as an analyst (actually as a barker) for the XFL telecasts orchestrated by Vince McMahon, the promoter whose pro wrestling vaudeville gave Ventura his first forum. XFL is a football league that aggressively tries to justify its label as minor league. The wardens of bedrock political values in Minnesota—principles that thrust Hubert Humphrey and Walter Mondale into presidential politics—are uniformly outraged by what they see as Ventura's sleazy misuse of the office. But they do give him credit for changing the main street dialogue in Minnesota. It used to be that when two Minnesotans got together they talked about the snow depth after the last blizzard. They now talk about the latest burlesques coming out of the office of their governor, as though some of Ventura's nuttiness has become a state resource to replace winter storms and Lake Wobegon.

All of which may explain The Body's continued popularity in Minnesota, and obscure the fact that he was elected by a third of the voters in a three-way race. A lot of those who didn't vote for him accept him with a kind of shrugging forgiveness: He may be an embarrassment but he hasn't been a disaster. In fact, some of his grades are impressive. His appointments to important commission offices have been sound. His damage control advisor, John Wodele, who's in charge of putting a negotiable spin on some of Ventura's loonier flights of logic, is expert. Ventura has put himself on the side of good government by advancing the cause of light rail in the Twin Cities and raising barriers against the manipulation of taxpayers by stadium-promoting athletic teams.

But his espousal of the old rugged individualist themes— "Do it yourself, man,"—chills people who know that life isn't that simple or available to multitudes of poor and voiceless people. It especially puts at risk future students whose education is imperiled by his ideas of shrinking the budget of the struggling University of Minnesota. Nor do friends of the school who are proud of its medical and technical breakthroughs take any comfort from a hardball governor who makes big dough on the side.

What he is as governor is what he was before: a pro wrestler who made it big with a hammerhead style and a hustler's brass. Bob Whereat, a *Minneapolis Star Tribune* reporter, looked at the Jackal badge he was told to wear and said he wouldn't. "The jackal business is silly but I'm offended by the implication that I might not be allowed to cover a news conference if I didn't write what the governor approves." In retrospect, Wodele said, that wasn't the intent.

But Ventura got to be a pro wrestling star in a business where villains had to be invented. Jesse is no Nero. He may have less power but more craft. If you're a wrestler-politician looking for a villain, the newsroom is an irresistible pigeon. In Minnesota, the folks who work with editors, keyboards and crystal balls are as confounded by Ventura as the public.

The Marketers of War
Decide Which Americans Are Patriots

June 2004

In the midst of the war in Vietnam, a time when I wrote a daily column for the *Minneapolis Star*, I sometimes telephoned the family of a Minnesota man killed in the fighting. Three or four times I attended the funeral service or the rites in the cemetery.

The survivors answered my questions with whatever courtesy they could summon from the depth of their desolation. I wrote of their anguish but also their pride. Where it seemed right, I tried to reconstruct the young man's life, to explore his fears and whimsies and his visions of a world without the daily scent of death. I quoted from his letters reluctantly, because each time I turned a page it seemed a clumsy invasion. And yet the family said, "We'd like to share these." It was their way of telling the world of their unbreakable commitment to him and their love. They seemed to be saying: he was a fine young man who had so much to give; we treasured him then and we treasure him now. But he was so young.

I grieved with the family as the flag-covered coffin was lowered. The soldier who'd lost his life had been drafted to fight, or he'd volunteered. It didn't seem important at the cemetery how he acquired the uniform. At the requiems, I thought of what we'd shared. We had grown up in a part of America we both knew well and whose ideas of social fairness seemed to make sense. We had worn the same uniform. We were somehow together.

It never occurred to me that in order to grieve for the victims of war I had to agree with the purposes of the war or why and how it was waged.

I thought it was highly unlikely that all of its victims had. It never occurred to me that in order to be counted an honorable citizen of the country, one had to give robotic support to the behavior of the government waging the war.

But today we have Iraq. We have a presidential election. We've been handed new rules about what constitutes star-spangled, dipped-in-apple-sauce patriotism. It means let Karl Rove and Fox News decide how loyal you are to America. It means buy Donald Rumsfeld's baloney. It means you can't claim to support the American troops in Iraq unless you keep George Bush in the White House.

This is what's being piped into the political commercials.

It didn't occur to me that there was any contradiction between being (a) an American citizen infuriated by being systematically lied to and manipulated by the government on the life-and-death issues of war, and (b) being an American citizen who could still mourn the death of young American soldiers in Iraq.

In the marketing of the war in Iraq, and in the high-stakes sound bites of a presidential election, there is a rising and disgusting innuendo: if you don't like how we got into Iraq and why, you have to be privately cheering those mounting body counts.

That's the equation. You're giving aid and comfort to terrorists if you harbor a suspicion that the government may actually have something to hide by trying to tar Richard Clarke and the rest of the talking insiders who seem to have the goods.

The war was sold—in third or fourth incarnation of why America started a war—as an indispensable step to eradicate terror. What it has done is to expand the terror. But the newest strategy of its promoters is to paint you as a moral outcast, a jellied wimp, if you wonder out loud about the spreading bloodshed and shambles in Iraq and raise questions about who drew this aimless blueprint and where is it taking us.

Under the new rules of patriotism and fearless Americanism, talking that way means you want us to cut and run in Iraq.

That's the picture the marketers of the war are trying to create to salvage the election. That is the new definition of what you're doing if you say you don't trust the people who are running the government as though it's a private inner sanctum guarded by wolfhounds and Dick Cheney's contractors.

There is no middle ground there. If you think there might have been a better way in Iraq, a way to avoid getting a thousand more Americans killed after George Bush landed unopposed on the flight deck of an aircraft carrier, you're saying we ought to cut and run.

If you think there had to be a better way to obliterate and occupy Iraq, without theatrically humiliating the United Nations before it happened, then you're saying we ought to cut and run. In today's Washington, those are the new rules of engagement if you want to win your stripes as a patriotic citizen.

If you believe there might have been a way to avoid killing thousands of Iraqi innocents, then you're saying to the arbiters of patriotism: it wasn't worth the slaughter; they were human beings, too. The answer from the White House comes with a thunderclap of indictment: you're a bleating heart, a whipped dog and probably a subversive.

If you express contempt for the evasions, duplicity and secrecy that constitute the modus operandi of today's government in Washington, then you're saying we ought to bug out of Iraq.

In fact, you're saying no such thing. In fact, not many people are. Even if you wanted to, it's a delusion that the USA can cut and run. We're embedded there. We're embedded because we put out a contract to change the regime, to oversee the distribution of Iraq's oil, to eventually reshape the Middle East, and to elect George in November.

That is the scenario. We can dispose of the argument about the real purposes of the war in Iraq. That's not going to be unraveled in time for November of 2004 let alone November of 3004. It felt reassuring to go to war at a time when we were 45 minutes away from mass destruction. It turns out there had to be other reasons.

What those reasons were is interesting but not compelling at this point. What matters now is to put enough soldiers and airmen and marines into Iraq long enough to establish some law and order, to separate the maniacal insurgents from the sane insurgents, to stop the killing and to wait for November. There's only one fundamental question the American people need to answer then: Who do you trust most to level with you about what the government is doing with your lives and your children's future?

If the answer is the incumbent president, then the country should not complain about where it's going.

John Kerry and a
Rainy Day in Rochester

October 27, 2004

It rained hard and relentlessly today where I live. The rainstorm seemed to deepen the solemnity of the approaching day of decision for America, made it look grim.

Well, maybe that's an augury.

The day before, October 26, 2004, we drove down from Minneapolis to Rochester, Minnesota, the city of the Mayo Clinic, the citadel of health care and of medical miracles. For thousands of people around the world, it has become a wellspring for the renewal of life.

The campaign of John Kerry chose Rochester for one of his final major appearances before the election, notwithstanding the city's recent tradition as one of the rural fortresses of conservative Republicanism. The idea was to demonstrate that Kerry and some of the battered but still-lofty ideals of the Democratic Party can rally other voices in the midst of rural America.

It rained in Rochester, too. But they came by the thousands, from southern Minnesota, northern Iowa, Minneapolis and St. Paul. They filled the 7,500-seat Mayo Civic Auditorium and spilled over into the adjacent grounds. Not all of them came spontaneously. Presidential political rallies of the twenty-first century aren't conducted with crossed legs and worried looks at the horizon for symptoms of sunlight. Newly-naturalized Somali women were shuttled to the rally from the Twin Cities. Hundreds of young people who sat near them didn't pop up impulsively out of the cornfields. But none of them came reluctantly. And if you were one of those approaching the dignified status of an old crock of American politics, it was impossible not to be lit up by the concentrated exuberance of the crowd. It could have been one of Hubert Humphrey's dusk-to-dawn bean feeds in the old Minneapolis Auditorium. It had almost the identical blow-out atmospherics and cheek-to-cheek camaraderie. All that was missing was somebody's Better Than Dirt amateur band playing "Happy Days Are Here Again."

The atmospherics were almost identical, but not quite.

This was not a political rally of the mid-1900s when, whatever the decision of election day, the country was going to return to an acceptable political peace and to an America as usual.

This is an America that truly believes in the dominant mantra rising from the clamor and the gut-kicking of the campaign of 2004, and in some ways from a lurking dread: That this is the most important election of our lifetimes.

It certainly is the most dangerous.

Dangerous because the country has been tearing itself apart politically in a clash of competing values, so virulent that it has by now persuaded most Americans that the bedrock of their democracy—the idea of an honest election—may be corrupted.

They have a right to be scared or suspicious. From the burlesque in Florida in 2000 to the chaotic stampede to harvest or block new voter registration this year, there's plenty of evidence that election fraud can be creatively engineered. So we have the spectacle today of armies of lawyers and poll watchers from both sides about to storm the polling places. Some of them we'll want to thank for protecting legally certified voters. We'll suspect others of shielding the imposters. Election day disruption is predictable. The hostage in all of this is the country's trust in the one irreplaceable doctrine of American democracy—the honest election.

That is a shadow hanging over Tuesday. Another is the real possibility that the oligarchy that now runs America will, by winning this election, declare a mandate to continue its recklessness into the unlimited future. This is a government that works in virtual blood-oath secrecy, has needlessly killed thousands of innocents thousands of miles away, has run a war with arrogant incompetence and presided over the theft of billions of dollars from its own citizens to enrich billionaires. In the process it has cost its citizens millions of jobs, reduced their health care and earning power and virtually crippled American public education.

So I went to hear John Kerry in Rochester, and I sat in a section behind the stage wearing a small badge reading "Veteran for Kerry-Edwards," bearing a tiny sub-title, "for a stronger America."

I think I would have said for a better America. America is strong enough. It is rich enough. It is not as good as it should be, or as it once was. People who may have traveled less tell me "Everybody around the world hates us." Well, they don't. Americans are generally held as fondly as they were ten and fifteen years ago. Americans individually remain generous and open. It isn't Americans that are detested around the world. It is the behavior of the American government today that people find appalling. It is a government that has alienated most of the civilized world with its belligerence in avenging 9/11, its posturing as the conscience and the warden of the world, and its hypocrisy as the knight of democracy and world order while it creates turmoil with its refusal to be a conciliator where it could produce legitimate and life-saving peace.

In Rochester, John Kerry said the usual Kerry things, and they were punchy and credible. This was a decent and thoughtful man finally finding his traction in the heavy lifting of this clangorous campaign. The crowd was alive and responsive. It was a comfort to sit there with good folks who looked so ready for a new breath in Washington. But under their layer of happy times ahead I know there was some festering worry about whether this can really happen. Kerry was confident and looked presidential. But so was George Bush a few hours later on my television set, deriding

Kerry's hip-shooting with the facts and the rest of the usual indictments.

Four more years of the obsessions of the Bush government, pandering to corporate power and greasing it, slickering an America public still wanting to believe in an American dream—I found that almost too loathsome to look at seriously in Rochester. So I sat at the Mayo Center while the Democrats got everybody through security and Carole King warmed up the crowd and Garrison Keillor got us through the introductions. I found myself drifting back into the politics of the 1960s. Did Kerry have the stuff to be another John Kennedy? Another Bill Clinton? Well, yes. Why not? I recycled John Kennedy. We had a connection, I remembered. It was not exactly historic but it pulled me back into what I thought was a better time for America. I remembered forty-four years ago, the day after the 1960 election. I was sitting at a typewriter in the Associated Press bureau in Minneapolis. It was nine a.m. and the world was clamoring for an American president. John Kennedy was six votes short of clinching the presidency. Illinois, California and Minnesota were still out. It those years the county auditors actually counted the votes and phoned them in to the two major wire services. George Moses, the bureau chief, and Adolph Johnson, the political writer, came over to my typewriter. I was writing the election leads for Minnesota and the Dakotas. Richard Nixon and Kennedy were running almost dead even in Minnesota. But the bulk of the Iron Range and Duluth votes—3 to 1 Democratic in those years—had not been tabulated.

The three of us talked. Nixon couldn't possibly match Kennedy on the Range and in Duluth. Moses called the general desk in New York. "We're going to elect Kennedy," he said. "I've got two words of advice," the chief of the general desk said. "Be right."

He hung up a number for us on the AP's trunk wire and I started writing. Moses pulled the copy out my machine a paragraph at a time. We didn't have time to slip carbons into the hard copy. After four paragraphs I yelled to the teletype operator, Bob Mexner: "How did that last paragraph end?" Mexner tried to be helpful. "With a period," he said.

The world had a president.

I was dawdling with that memory when Garrison Keillor cued the music in Rochester and led the crowd, 7,500 strong, in the national anthem. When it was over the woman next to me was crying—my wife, Susan Wilkes. "You know," she said. "It isn't only the people who noisily proclaim their patriotism who love this country. It's been so good for me, and for so many others."

It has that. It was an altogether marvelous country for my immigrant grandparents, who made a grail out of an education for their children and those who came after. I think most of those who were at Rochester know this country well enough to know when it's made a wrong turn. We will find out Tuesday whether there are enough Americans who have made the same judgment.

A Long Morning After

November 3, 2004

I waded uninvited into the gloom of a small office work crew at about the time of John Kerry's concession speech. The atmosphere oozed with subdued misery, evidently shared equally by the four or five employees.

It's awkward intruding on a scene of grief, especially when you have to add a few drabs of your own. I would have felt the same way walking into an opera a few moments after the soprano expired from consumption. I came on a minor business errand I'd been postponing for hours. I didn't feel any better than the employees or, when you think about it, than the soprano.

The customer's arrival may have interrupted their conversation. I couldn't tell. I wanted to ask if this was a private wake or could anybody get in. Somebody spotted my Kerry button and seemed relieved to drop the mask of nonpartisanship with a safe customer on the premises.

"I'm just so damned devastated by the election," he said. "I thought we were going to win it."

I did, too, but I don't know about devastated. Devastated sounds like something wholly and tragically irreversible, and politics is never that. But I had to join the deepening trauma around me until I remembered Adlai Stevenson's story after his loss to Dwight Eisenhower in their second election. Stevenson was asked how it felt being blown out a second time by the general. Adlai was a worldly guy, passionate about social justice but a thinker and a realist. He told of a farmer sitting in the debris of his house and outbuildings, all of them torn to bits by a tornado. A neighbor walked a mile to commiserate with him and found the farmer giggling unstoppably.

"What are you laughing at, you crazy fool," the neighbor asked. "Your place is a wreck."

"I'm laughing," he said, "at the completeness of it."

The Democrats weren't ripped to bits by the George Bush Republicans, so I'm not laughing through the gloom. They *were* left in shock because in the final days, feeling the adrenaline of a solidarity they had not experienced for years, the Democrats translated the dead-heat prophecies of the polls into a surging victory for their candidate.

There was nothing wrong with the Democratic candidate. This is a man of honor and judgment and proven guts who could have led the county out of its new isolation and imperialism. He was pilloried early in the campaign and some of the crud stuck. It wasn't only the Swift Boat Liars' slander against him that was offensive. It was the robotic arrogance with which they pressed their story. They came back into Minnesota in the last week of the campaign and in effect were telling Minnesotans: "We know this is garbage, but we're going to run these ads because we want to win and we think you're dumb enough to buy into it."

Some of the country was. Minnesota wasn't.

The late count in Ohio and the odd arithmetic of the electoral vote made it look a little closer than it was. But it was no sweep and no mandate. The country is still and angrily divided, with reason. It was fashionable among Democratic bean counters, in the final hours of the campaign, to picture the Bush adherents as people in denial.

At the time, it was the Democrats who were probably in denial. We called it the most important election in our lifetimes. In retrospect that has the sound of apocalypse now, and the temptation today may be to sweep it into the corner. If that was the election of a lifetime, what do we call 2006 and 2008 and beyond?

The language, in fact, may not have been far-fetched. We will know in the next four years and beyond. It will be then when we learn the price of the Bush government's mismanagement of the war it created, its paranoid secrecies, the horrific deficits it has run up for the sake of corporate and private enrichment, the gradual erosion of quality education in the public schools and of the social contract between government and its citizens. Onto this add the killing of tens of thousands of innocent civilians and more than a thousand American service men and women in a bizarre and needless war.

The election results didn't repeal those indictments against a reckless government. What they did was to affirm the reality of politics in America today. The Republicans have successfully lined up with aggressive, Bible-thumping armies of believers, with armies of hunters and sportsmen, with mainstream farmers and blue-collar workers who are appalled by the idea of writing gay and lesbian marriage into law.

To millions of Americans, being part of these multitudes is to wear the look of true blue Americans and to hold beliefs and animosities that have the feel of true American values. And some of them, in fact, *are* traditional American values.

And then all of those true blue colors turn to solid red on the electoral maps, from the South to the Midwest to the Southwest to the Mountain West, and the Democrats become enclaves trying to stay afloat against the tide.

And does that mean millions of Americans are voting against their economic interests, against their own yearnings for productive and healthy lives, and their belief in the preservation of strong public schooling?

It does. And when the man who identifies himself as the embodiment of all these values tells you he will protect you against terror by sending the American flag into Iraq, you are probably not going to vote against the American flag. A retired major general did make the point during the campaign—one that shouldn't have to be made—that baloney is baloney whether or not it's wrapped in the flag.

The building of the Republican base has been shrewd and sometimes ruthless, but that is called hardball politics and it is what the Republicans play far better than the Democrats, with assistance from the cable TV drumbeaters. They have been able to play it well and successfully because the Democrats years ago began paying the price for spreading their traditional umbrella of support wider as the appellant groups grew and began demanding their share of justice or a wedge of the democracy's pie. Their clients from the turn of the century began with labor and the poor and weak and voiceless and minorities and grew to women's rights and environmental rights. And then came gays and lesbians and now gay marriage. The Democrats have not officially espoused all of the demands, nor have all Democrats or even most of them. But Democrats became easy targets for politicians who tar them as tree-huggers, elitists, gun-confiscators and promoters of homosexuality.

That is sad and mostly abominable. Democrats invited it by being perceived as cavalier about what was offending Americans. But that is the politics of today and soon millions of people who once crowded under that umbrella no longer have need for it and can comfortably ignore those who do. Yet how does all of that explain Minnesota, which with Wisconsin defied the Republican farm belt sweep?

This isn't quite the Minnesota of Hubert Humphrey or the same old never-never land of happy liberalism. The Republicans hold much of the power in Minnesota today, but it is a Republicanism unlike the one remembered best by the builder Republicans who still vote. A half century ago, moderate Republicans and the new Democratic Farmer-Labor Party together built a political ethic in Minnesota that gave rise to some of the country's most progressive political and social concepts and movements. Corporate power and government cooperated in building world-renowned medicine and brain industries. The weak were cared for. Public health and education mattered. There were excesses but by and large the state worked. So the rankest appeals to partisanship and self-interest don't always fly in Minnesota. Thousands of once moderate Republicans voted for John Kerry. They included many of the most prominent ones, who did it in the closet. Minnesota is a state where strong minded women are not exactly unknown. Many of those, in essentially Republican, suburban households, voted for Kerry. College students got involved. And Kerry delivered his calls for a new turn in American politics, and a new awareness of our need for friends around the world, to thundering ovations the last week in Minnesota.

As a citizen of this state, I take some comfort in Tuesday. But I take more in the sight of those aroused young people, finding a cause, discovering that they could invest their energies in something beyond their own needs and ambitions. And not only in the young people, but in grandmas walking with canes, and in veterans who know something about guts and sacrifice, standing proud with John Kerry.

I was proud to stand with them.

A Mighty New America
—But Less Than It Was

February 2005

In the *New York Times* of February 2, 2005, the inside pages, I found a story from a suddenly wealthy but uneasy Ireland. It presented one those dicey enigmas of life that think tank gurus love to bat around: how high is the potential price of glory and transformation?

It's not hard to get started gnawing on those calculations. Kings, generals and quarterbacks sometimes ignore them and pay the price of oblivion. What had me wondering was the transformation of a country, specifically my own, in my lifetime. Where is it going? Does it remember its fundamental strengths, derived decades ago from the struggles of its people. Has it learned enough from where it's been? Has it learned enough about Rome, Greece and Egypt or, for that matter, the Soviet Union, to say nothing of the Wall Street Catastrophe of 1929?

Does it remember, or care, how it dreamed and acted when it was at its best, its worthiest and its most admired?

Have we entered a time when the public is so skillfully manipulated and duped that its government now feels comfortable following this chilling political vector, in the words of a White House advisor to author Ron Suskind:

"We're an empire now, and when we act, we create our own reality…We're history's actors…and you, all of you, will be left to just study what we do."

Their own reality, dressed and cleaned up so it becomes our reality.

And when the White House interpreters speak, in run-ups to the wars it's planning, to the new exclusionary laws it's framing, to the elections it needs to win, is that what we're getting, "our own reality" in the place of the truth?

In other words, the citizens are being told that what they're seeing is not what is but what the government says it is. Not our blunders and grandiosity but "bad intelligence;" not corporate America seizing control of the country again to amass new wealth, but "tax cuts to fuel the economy;" not repealing the partnership between the people and its government but "getting the government off the people's back."

The piece on Ireland told of sudden and record prosperity there—something for which that struggling little country has yearned for hundreds of years. But prosperity has come with a price—rising divorce rates, increased drug use and higher crime rates.

When I finished the *Times* piece on Ireland I added another of the old mantras of human ambition and obsession: be careful what you wish for.

Many American citizens are not sure where we ought to go with success. The Irish may have an advantage there. They don't have nuclear bombs, thirty red states and late-arriving urges to run the world.

On that proposition, the political partisans as well as the political scholars were at each other's throats during the 2004 presidential election campaign. Anger stoked by a sense of futility hung over half of the American population like a darkening storm. America's post-9/11 solidarity in grief and shared purpose quickly dissolved when a lust for war laced with huge tax cuts for the wealthy and budget slashes for essential services became part of a new White House template for the idyllic society. By then Americans were doing some serious reflection about the future. Was fear, they asked themselves, going to be part of daily life indefinitely now that America was exposed to fanatics? And what was the best way to reduce that fear?

Well, Al-Qaeda was in Afghanistan so let's go into Afghanistan.

That made sense to almost everybody. And Iraq?

The president said Saddam was evil and ready to use poison gas against us or worse. Tony Blair said it could happen in 45 minutes. Colin Powell put on a show at the United Nations. The president walked up a regal red carpet to address the people of American, and it was war in Iraq. That easy.

I was one of the Americans who thought it shouldn't be that easy. It shouldn't be so smooth that the country would willingly accept a new king-of-the-hill America that announced to the world: We've got the biggest bombs, the most money and we're going to do the talking from here on. If you want to listen and join the club, you're our pals and you'll get invited to a barbecue at the Crawford. If you don't, change you're mailing address to Dogpatch, Mongolia, and we'll call you in five or ten years.

But, I thought, is this really Armageddon here and now, the supreme crisis in the history of humanity? Is this the first time our security has been seriously threatened in modern times, so that in order to face it we have to re-invent America and act like a stomping Godzilla of the video games? And if it's that much of a crisis, why are we burglarizing the American treasury in broad daylight by turning millionaires into billionaires with these horrendous tax cuts?

Most of us lived through the Cold War from start to finish. Each day offered the possibility of a global conflagration in which the mushrooms from hundreds of exploding nuclear bombs could transform our country, the Soviet Union and the world into an into an end-of-civilization graveyard.

We averted it without bombast, but not without strength when it came to eleventh hour decisions and steady nerves at the center of power in this country.

But now, you have to begin the day wearing a mental flak jacket because it's never going to be clear what is truth and what is smokescreen when the government speaks in Washington. You're in doubt whether the government is serving its people or some grand and wacko scheme of remaking the world and then dismantling the public's safety nets to pay for the grandiosity and incompetence. You also have to ask a question: have we been re-formed into a permanently belligerent, fist-shaking America, mocking the advocates of restraint and piling up enemies by the millions around the world? And in domestic politics, have we entrenched a power-thirsty crowd guided by the managers of money and the defenders of privilege, entranced by guns, gospel-singers, gas-devouring machines on the highway and, in fact, subsidizing the owners of those machines?

I'm a child of the Depression of the 1930s. Our home was in a mining town in northern Minnesota. What I remember about the Depression, apart from the worried faces and the daily struggle, was the stolid trust the people placed in the government in a time of their deepest torment. It wasn't a blind, unconditional acceptance. Struggling for survival doesn't lend itself to hugs-and-kisses attitudes. It was closer to a feeling that there was some distant, gray presence somewhere out there, in a time of the nation's bankruptcy, trying to be a public servant. That distant force made some monumental mistakes. But I don't remember any real suspicion that we were being lied to or maneuvered. I don't recall having any doubts that eventually we would work our way out of the hard times.

We know now that World War II eventually hastened the end of the hard times. But we also know that true democratization of America grew out of the landmark legislation and temper of the 1930s and 1940s, the Social Security program, the 40-hour work week, the development of the labor union movement, safety laws and much more. The once powerless acquired a voice. They began to earn enough money to buy clothes and to put more food on the table and, in time, to send their children to college.

Since that time, our land has become immensely rich and the most powerful ever.

But there are times today when to millions of its citizens the country has the look of a strange and different America, applauded by other millions who embrace what seem to be new and delusionary political commandments. Like what? That wilderness protections are foolish intrusions on America's entrepreneurial spirit; that whatever works in sustaining the new overlords of America, no matter how ruthless and defamatory the tactic, is OK; that the American president is very likely working God's will; and if all of that sounds alien to you, you don't understand the new American mission in the world.

It's not that the America of my earlier years was notably gentler or gifted with wisdom of the ages. America has always been a pretty volatile place. It went through a Civil War, stole land from the Indians and loosed thugs against union organizers. Its heinous suppression of minorities fueled race riots. And it then found itself fighting a generational and anti-war rebellion in the 1960s.

That's an impressive inventory of ugliness. But through the decades this tempestuous country had grown wiser. It has become aware not only of its bounty but also of its responsibility to build and advance the lives of the less privileged of its citizens, through the courts, through legislation, and by the simple recognition that it was the right thing to do. In fact, this became the core moral value of the American society, at least a sizable part of that society—to distribute its wealth and energy in a way that permitted a dignified life for the least able among its people. Over time our society demonstrated that it could be prudent in managing resources and careful in the exercise of power. It could tax the rich and the expanding middle class on their ability to pay, and as a result, the nation paids its bill with something approaching fairness. As it evolved, our society demonstrated that it could reward initiative and skill without neglecting the struggles of the poor and, later, the injustice inflicted on women.

It wasn't utopia, but what I've described is approximately what America became late in the twentieth century, after all of its ordeals of Civil War, World Wars, the depression, racism, Viet Nam, correcting the worst excesses of the welfare state and a hundred related turmoils that pepper the history of this extraordinary country.

And then shortly after the millennium turned, we found ourselves in the middle of a frenzied reversal. It was a calculated full court press to roll back some of those remarkable advances in equalizing opportunity, protecting the citizens' rights in court and on the street, and curbing the vast power of the corporate juggernaut in America.

The seminal event that opened the gates for it was the terrorist attack of 9-11. Between then and in the ensuing runup events to the 2004 presidential election the emerging Republican powerhouse seemed inflamed with the mission of carrying the American flag to all available continents or forcing it there or buying our way in with payoffs. The American leadership drew on the country's fears of another terror attack and invoked the public's patriotric duty to support the troops because, the scenario went, they were defending America by attacking Iraq. The nation's reporters and photographers were imbedded with the advancing forces. They were to tell the story of an America launching its unprecedented firepower to assert its strength and its righteousness. In the process, the government's mouthpieces and its president belittled the United Nations and other international councils. It scorned the inspectors' reports, which said no weapons of mass destruction had been uncovered in Iraq. The message from America was blunt. Out of our way. We want the world to approve what we're doing and join in to help us, but we really don't much care if it doesn't.

So we invaded Iraq on flimsy and bogus charges, killed tens of thousands of innocent Iraqi people who we had promised to save with our invasion, and later told their next of kin they were now free as pledged.

In the process of confronting radical Islam, the Bush administration rounded up hundreds of people we called enemy combatants. They were imprisoned without trial and in effect told they could rot there for the rest of there lives unless they could prove their innocence, which they could hardly attempt because they were denied due process.

We spent billions of dollars destroying Iraq, billions of dollars more occupying it and billions more trying to reconstruct obliterated cities. Our government gave egregious profits to contractors, ate up more billions gobbling up budget surpluses left over from the 1990s and amassed monster deficits. This was done in part by granting billions of dollars in tax relief to the richest people in America—in the midst of unprecedented military spending.

During this time of runaway extravagance by the mightiest and richest nation in world history, we discovered that 47 million Americans had no health coverage, more than 30 million lived under the poverty line, 11 million kids were uninsured and some schools were reducing classes to four days a week because they were running out of money

Scholars in the conservative think tanks said projecting our military power around the world, fueling the economy by giving tax breaks to corporate entrepreneurs and deregulating industry, including communication giants, were prudent ways to protect America's interests.

All of this, to me and 50 million or other Americans, looked like sanitized cover for what was really happening: a counter-revolution to repeal the New Deal of the 1930s and successive Democratic administrations that lifted millions of the previously ignored and exploited into the middle class. The result was to re-energize America and transform it into an honest-to-God democracy.

But in just a couple of years, empowered by the legalized theft of a presidential election in 2000, a crowd of smart and vengeful right wing apparatchicks put corporate power back at the controls of America and the Pentagon in charge of the world.

Massive sums of money were raised by the U.S. Chamber of Commerce, the insurance industry and other economic powerplants to lobby Congress for laws that suited the purposes of the White House and the industries. All that money constituted an investment, buying quick access to the White House. It's a highly chummy and profitable arrangement that is off-limits to the average citizen and outsider groups, who have no access at all.

The government in power today is not partial about choosing its partners. It allied itself equally with religious hosts, who get financial breaks from a grateful White House and Congress. It froze out minority Democrats from any serious role in the critical congressional decisions, and it invested millions of dollars in campaigns to defeat or discredit the more influential ones. Its goal was not only to defeat the Democratic Party but to destroy it as a meaningful force in American politics. The canniest political manipulators ever installed in Washington have managed to convince a majority of the American people, at least during the political campaigns, that war is peace. War and the threat of war are said to be the only guarantor peace and happy times. The scenario of establishing global control was widened. a) We are the mightiest power on earth. b) We are going to be sure nobody challenges us. c) War and the threat to make war give us the most persuasive tools to move the world where we want it moved. d) If we need somebody else's land to base our fire power, we can protect America and achieve our God-supported goals with a selective use of an old Mafia-style strategy: give those little countries an offer they can't refuse.

The broader picture the American public was receiving day in and day out went like this: We are a good and powerful people, but this new war (on terror) is endless. It demands that Americans rally around the commander-in-chief and consider him a hero of our times. The people who say "Try diplomacy, it might save lives" are the faint-hearted who don't understand America. Worse, they may say something good about France. But you can trust your president.

The political handlers and producers in Washington have studied history carefully. They recognize that sometimes the public needs and craves distractions. It needs reminders that its leaders are not only sure-handed but prophetic and the creators of epic events. When the president needs to address the world, don't prop him at a desk in front of a camera and wait until the light goes red. He should be seen making a long and solemn walk on a red carpet and then emerge larger than life, attended by a phalanx of American flags, to make his historic announcements. When the public needs a feel-good moment, the producers recognize that bread and circuses have been done before with mixed results. More photogenic are extravagant arrivals on an aircraft carrier in full flight regalia.

The choreographers of this new era of dazzle-and-dupe understand that the people need to be guided in how they think. This means truth must be doled out in limited portions. If necessary, the truth should be strangled when that seems more practical. The public doesn't have to be clued into all that's going on behind the transoms in the new-era government. It should stop worrying about monopolies and even bigger words like oligarchies. It should favor huge consolidations and mergers which, after all, increase efficiency and stock option bonuses by reducing jobs, eliminating pensions and stifling the last breath of air from the unions.

And by the way, there's another role of the new-era government that the public might not understand since it's been numbed by the administration's fog machines. The best way to neuter the regulatory departments that protect the people's rights and living conditions is to appoint agency directors who know how to destroy the agency. This was neatly done between 2000 and 2004. As a testament to the artistry of the president's handlers, most of the public didn't realize it, and most of the media folks didn't report it.

Now these people have their sensitivities and they admit it's sad what happened in rural America, to the family farms and the country stores since the corporate farm industries wiped them out with their huge subsidies. But the commonfolk should still count their blessings and options. There is always a Wal-Mart somewhere in the county with its quaint 19th century policies of cheap labor and tight-fisted benefits to hold down prices and remind America how lucky it is to get rid of those boxy little family shops that have disappeared by the thousands since the Wal-Mart bulldozers came.

I have bicycled through scores of little towns or villages in Minnesota that are no longer there, except for a gas station, a saloon, deserted barns and elevators and a creaking beer sign on the edge of town. I suppose some of that is inevitable. But if you have lived more than 70 years as I have, you know that we are coming a little closer each year to the creation of a Giganticus Americanus. You can't do much about the new tempos of life and cultures of life. There is a round the clock vulgarity on television, a deification of the violence in professional football and the creation a whole pantheon of Midas Gods who play the games, some of whom rail at their $10 million salaries as an offense against their families, who need to be fed and clothed.

But you can't credibly deny that life for the workaday American is a lot more convenient, quirky, thrilling and mobile. People make business deals looking at their new partners face to face across 3,000 miles on TV hookups. You can hold an electronic marvel in your hand, talk to somebody halfway around the world for 10 cents, listen to 2000 hours of music if you have the time, read three newspapers on a two inch screen and pay the rent, without recharging the batteries. All of that is miraculously goofy and irresistible, and it does make life good and suspenseful, but something stops me before I want to call it the glorious America of the 21st Century.

What stops me is that the government of America is mindlessly squandering so much of our wealth and energy today in a paranoid attempt to make the country fearsome and invincible. It refuses to recognize the difference between an America powerful and an America omnipotent, which it is not and can't be. If America's power brokers don't understand that, their successors may when China's economic and military power equal ours. What we have had for the last few years is a clique of American political commissars embarked on a transparent scheme to permanently lock-in political and economic power in the hands of an ideological junta and its corporate allies. All of this is astronomically expensive and it would be at least fathomable if the operation were in the hands of competent people. The sad evaluation of its competence is that the one truly brilliant mind in control belongs to the behind-the-curtains Gepetto, Karl Rove, who has made most it happen, including Bush.

As for the cost of it, the manipulators have lied and misled in their estimates, performing astonishing tricks with the numbers to keep the taxpayers dumbed down, the Congress in line, and future generations in debt

But—

After unburdening, it's a good idea to tell yourself that the United States of America is, after all, resilient and gifted with unusual powers of self-preservation. You can't survive the Redcoats, droughts, depressions, floods, vaudeville, halftime at the Super Bowl and 360 television channels without being resilient. I tried to explain that to my fellow grievers at the wailing wall they erected after the November 2 election in 2004. They wanted to know what was left after Kerry lost. I said, well, it's bad, but how about tomorrow? That's a start.

The start is the knowledge that historically, there's a yin and yang to politics in America, which probably reflects the strength of the country's peculiar two-party system. And the ebbs and flow of it eventually will discredit the political monstrosity we're seeing today. Now and then on the highway, driving through an especially lovely part of rural Minnesota, I tell myself, "You lucky stiff." I remind myself that I have lived fully one third of the life span of the United States of America, and I have seen this country at its very best, when it has been truly generous, when it has faced the horrors of the Depression and then the shock of Pearl

Harbor and the ultimate challenge of World War II and the Cold War. I remind myself that our governments are run by politicians, who sometimes deserve the confidence of their voters and sometimes are frail, venal or wrongheaded. Not many combine the qualities of recklessness, cunning and deviousness and still manage to draw cheers from 60 million people. The country will know when it's time for a change, assuming it is not bankrupted before that time comes.

None of it has diminished my thanksgiving for having lived in America, for being an American and having received the gift of opportunity in America. I learned to love this country and the people I saw in it when it was its poorest.

Those who said after 9-11 that there was never a time in America when it's solidarity was so powerfully and intimately felt. Perhaps. It was a traumatic event, bringing America together from ocean to ocean. But in the Depression, in small town America, the people, neighborhoods, came together, solemnly and unbreakably, in a way that transcended neighborhood itself. It was something closer to Biblical togetherness, your brother's keeper.

We had two or three Jewish merchants in the mining town where I grew up. Anti-Semitism was not unknown then. People called Jews "kikes" called African-Americans "niggers," although they only saw them when an all-black baseball team came to town. It was the way America was. People who accepted that language without speaking out, and remember it, are ashamed today. In those years, nearly a century ago, the Jewish merchants knew what was being said. If they probed deeper, they knew that most of the Scandinavians and Slavs and English and Italians who talked that way were probably decent enough people. They knew also that these people paid their bills and were courteous enough in the stores. And then the Depression struck, and in time their regular customers would come into a clothing store, Mike Gordon's or Phil Rosenbloom's, and ask if they could buy a pair of winter boots or a jacket, but they weren't working and couldn't pay right now.

"When you were working you always paid," the merchant would say, making a statement rather then asking the question.

"Yes," the customer would say.

"You can buy the boots," the merchant would say. "You can pay when you're working again."

There were no billing statements, no interest charges, no superfluous acknowledgements like "Your credit is good." It was understood. The months went by, and when the miner was working again, on the day he received his check he walked into the store and paid for his boots.

Words like "kike" disappeared from the town's vocabulary.

It was one way in which small America survived the Depression, and how America grew. When Franklin Roosevelt wanted to talk to the country, he made what he called fireside chats. Most people could afford a radio. He was a politician almost without equal and he was no benevolent godfather. But he was a leader. He didn't talk a lot of economics. He talked as intimately as an unseen president could over a scratchy radio wave, and he talked directly without being melodramatic. His idea was to re-build the gutted confidence of an America racked by dust bowls, bank foreclosures, lines of jobless, and hunger.

There could have been riots and civil war if Roosevelt had been just one more slick politician palming the deck, trying to get by. Rather, he told Americans what they were facing and how the government would try to help. I sat beside the wood stove, my mother and father in front of the Philco. They, like most Americans, believed they were getting a fair picture of where the country stood. FDR had a huge majority in the Congress and produced scheme after scheme—the WPA, the NRA, PWA, CCC, bank holidays, the works. Some helped, others flopped and a few were snuffed out by the Supreme Court. FDR wasn't averse to his own brazen schemes of roughshod power to get the country moving. He proposed expanding the Supreme Court's complement of nine justices with six of his own appointees to uproot the conservative character of the court. The plan, thank God, died ingloriously. The country slowly headed forward. Some of Roosevelt's ideas became the bedrock of our social protections and the inspirations for others, and 70 years later we moved into the 21st Century with prosperity unimagined by all of the prophets of economics.

American military power circled the world. The country was healthy. Social Security was in place and needed some tweaking from time to time. Medicare and Medicade needed more revision, but they deserved their place in the catalogues of old age protection. The promises of pensions for retiring workers were still part of the package, although for thousands of workers they abruptly disappeared in the mania of mergers and consolidation. On the other hand, IRA accounts and 401-Ks had burgeoned in the white hot economy of the 1990s. The abuses the country had inflicted on its minorities and disadvantaged had been largely recognized—not without the rebellion of the victims—and at least partially rectified. It was beginning to be a country in which all of us had some form of ownership, well before the label became popular.

Four years into the twenty-first century, a lot of those rational codes of national behavior and legacies were either under assault or on their way to burial. The people presiding over the upheaval pelted Americans with a drumfire of explanations. Government was overspending. And the worst spenders in history, of course, were the new spenders who beat the drums for prudence. When they cut public services, the richest in the land were spared the sacrifices. The people who paid for the new America were the poorest and the lower middle class, the school pupils and the men and women who tried to give them an education that would enable their kids to compete with the rich.

It was a losing battle. It was the New America, delivering

the worst blows on the heads of those least able to withstand them, lying about the cost to future America, passing onto our grandchildren the bill for their profligacy.

That is the difference between the America of today and the wounded but conscionable America in which I grew up, and the prosperous and expanding but still conscionable America in which I lived lived most of my adulthood.

In this process we are creating a new underclass. And that infuriates me both because it is totally wrong and unnecessary and because I remember the immigrant ideal of more than 70 years ago.

Scholars in the more liberal think tanks, during today's era of the bulldozing of the American idea, have not been completely buffaloed or silent. Their argument has been this: pre-emptive military strikes, empire building, squeezing public service, weakening or destroying protections for the environment, for clean air and water are presenting the country with a crisis that endangers the American society not only in the future but today. Attempts to dismantle Bill of Rights protections and ignoring the red flags of mounting deficits that threaten basic services are not kind of policies that created the great democracy and a respect for it around the world.

And how do Americans truly react to all these arguments about where we're headed?

Obviously, it is a mixed picture today. The polls have told us consistently since 2000 that the country is divided on both the means and the character, the actual motives, of the government in power. The strength of the Bush movement has been constant, right at or slightly above 50 per cent. Those opposed are not solidly opposed, but mostly opposed. Some of them are annoyed that a Democratic party that might have unhorsed the Bush clans in 2004 got dragged into fiascos like gay marriage, a fiasco because gay rights are one thing and gay marriage is another. It may be critical to some people but to most it is not.

The liberal scholars worry that they are witnessing

an America that is less than it once was and, for all of its unchallengeable might, may be a vanishing America.

I'm not a scholar of American economic and societal trends. I'm an American citizen, now in his 70s, who has seen and felt its strengths and admired its fundamental purposes and witnessed its generosity.

I also believe that it is an America that, today, is an America less than it once was.

It is less because in one of the deepest crises America has ever experienced, the Depression of the 1930s, the America government forged a partnership with its people. The partnership was imperfect. But for two or three generations, at least, it seemed to hold together in the creation of a society in which both government and the public understood they had a mutual goal—to better the conditions under which ALL Americans lived.

Today, in the midst America's greatest wealth and influence, that partnership has been assailed by deceit and crises that are partly self-inflicted or invented.

Except for two years in the Army, I've lived in Minnesota all of my life. I'm a grandson of immigrants from the Balkans, whose men worked for 10 and 12 hours a day in underground iron ore mines, sometimes not seeing the sun for days. They didn't cry about it. America for them meant work. It meant school for their children. It meant a new beginning. Education for their kids was the godhead of their lives. In Slovenia where my grandparents grew up, the Austrian authorities who then ruled Slovenia would line up the children in the village street in September, and choose one of ten to receive an education. This was more than a hundred years ago, but recent enough for the grandchildren of those immigrants to remember the stories. The iron mines were both a salvation and a kind of economic deadend for both the immigrants and the first generation that followed. But the mines fed the families and generated the money to buy clothes and to send the children to school.

This became the progression: My father went into the mines at the age of 15 because his parents both died of cancer and he had seven brothers and sisters to feed and clothe. There were no safety nets. His schooling ended in the eighth grade because he now had to become the family provider. My mother, also the daughter of immigrants, finished high school. A generation later, my brother and I attended the University of Minnesota. And the generation after that: one of my daughters attended Yale and the other a college in Iowa and graduated summa cum laude, and my brother's daughters also attended college. This brief history is not offered as a litany of familial success. It was the immigrant ethic of America, and it happened from ocean to ocean. Where I lived, the mines were both the crucible and the salvation in immigrants' deliverance. For years the men worked like moles, exploited in their early years. Because the safety rules were loose then, there were accidents and, for some of the men, the mines that had been their liberation from the oblivion of the old world became their tombs.

But that was the America of then. Until the early twentieth century it wasn't a world power. It didn't shake the courts of Europe. It was a curiosity and a market and something to watch. From the beginning America had been restless, reaching and grabbing for frontiers and horizons. But it would be decades before the kings and diplomats and generals worried about the it. It had enormous potential, ambitions, vast mineral wealth, an accelerating industry—but what it had above all was the energy and dreams and belief of the people who worked its factories, plowed its farmlands, and built its schools. The ultimate source of its strength, its greatest gift— even when the American gentry scorned it—was its diversity, in its faces, tongues, and drives.

I looked at that great gift a number of years ago and found it in the face of my grandmother, Rose, and, of course, thousands could do the same for thousands of grandmothers.

I once wrote:

On the Iron Range, and over a wider geography than that, she was an Everywoman of her time, the immigrant matriarch of the family. On the day my grandmother was buried in 1968, I drove from Minneapolis to Ely, where I was born, to attend the service. I gave thanks for what my grandmother had become for me, in her broken-English, harvesting pole beans in the yard, laughing through the sweat in eyes, an image of the whole glorious American idea. That idea could be summarized, I thought, by the lifetime of this woman who came out of the Slovenian highlands and landed on Ellis Island, scared but thrilled. I remembered her comforting breasts when I was a child. I remembered her sitting beside a funny black meat grinder, a babushka covering her bunned hair, her eyes full of smiles and wonder and delight when one of the grandchildren ran by and called her name. By the hour she churned out pork chunks and ran pointed pegs through the sausage ends to create ringlets that would be frozen and kept for the long northern winter. She never tired. Her hands were strong. Her bond with family was stronger.

She and the Finnish and Croatian and Jewish and Polish and Bulgarian and Italian and Sandinavian and German and English and Irish women and the women of a dozen other nationalities were priceless to the country's future, as the Latinos and Asians and Africans are today. In those years the immigrants were disgorged by the thousands, expecting no peppermint canes and lemon trees in the new country and without illusions about what lay ahead—leaky roofs and muddy streets in the mining towns, darkness in the pits for the men.

They were carried on the corporate books of the time as Cheap Labor. They might not have been aware of that, but it wouldn't have bothered them much if they had been. America was their redemption. It might laugh at their clumsy English and be scared by their foreign faces. But it would pay if they worked. It was huge and unstoppable, America. I didn't know what Grandma Rose's dreams were in the highlands before she left the old country. But after her death I explored what those dreams might have been and what her reality became. I never did decide what she imagined she would find or what she would become. Her husband, immigrated with her, worked underground for 30 years. His pension amounted to a few bucks week when he retired. He didn't feel used or underpaid. His kids went to school. He had food on the table and pin cherry wine in the basement. In some years it was Zinfandel wine, the years when he and a few hundred others in town contracted with the Casagrandes in Virgina for a load of Michigan grapes. It was legal, more or less, depending on how much wine you made. The cops didn't usually inquire, because the cops had some sizeable barrels in their own basements.

Grandma Rose gave me my first Christmas present and a grandmother's last embrace. She saw the country in terms of the bread and integrity it gave her family, in the beans and the dandelion salad they ate in the early years and something better as they grew older and the unions got stronger and the wages went up. The day after she died I said:

> "I don't think it occurred to her that the road ran two ways, that the genius and ultimate greatness of America flows more profoundly from the conflicts and struggles of its people than from its treasure; and by this measurement, one of its small but imperishable gifts came from the lady who spoke broken English and sang the songs of her native village. Most of the immigrants of the mining country are dead now or dying. On the Iron Range, the mines with their 12-hour work days of the 1920s first tyrannized them, but later welded a rough democracy among their sons and daughters.
>
> "Here for three or four decades was the essence of the American destiny—the meshing of the immigrants' hunger for identity with the nation's restless search for fulfillment. The mining headframes have been dismantled now and the

tunnels have been left to the echoes of the grinding winches and bantering miners. The old men on the hills have outlasted the pits that might have entombed them. My grandmother lived to see her youngest son become an internationally renowned scientist in the microchip field and a global lecturer. She lived to enjoy the modest luxury of a TV in her living room. In the fashion of the mining town society, she was the unquestioned conscience of her family. So there was no gold-paved street for the girl from the Balkan highlands. I don't know what she envisioned, but I do know what she meant to us. And her requiem is in the faces of the once-hungry who trusted her, and do not want today."

The great playwright, Arthur Miller, who died in 2005, understood, because he, too, was a child of the Depression.

A point arrived, he wrote in *Timebends*, sometime around 1936, "when for the first time unpolitical people began thinking of common action as a way out of their impossible conditions. Out of dire necessity came the surge of mass trade unionism and the federal government's first systematic relief programs, the resurgent farm cooperative movement, the Tennessee Valley Authority and other public projects that put people to work and brought electricity to vast new areas, repaired and built new bridges and aqueducts, carried out vast reforestation projects, funded student loans and research into the country's folk history—its songs and tales collected and published for the first time—and this burst of imaginative action created the sense of government that for all of its blunders and waste was on the side of the people."

History tells us that it was. The federal government we have had since 2000 has tried to create that illusion. No government in recent history has been as slick as this one in falsifying its intent.

The trust in America was all the immigrants brought to America, that and their ambitions. They became the nation's workers; their sons became its soldiers in World War II. And the immigrants died knowing that this trust—their contract with America—had not been betrayed. They died with the comforting knowledge that their children had been educated and could go as far in this marvelous land as their energies and choices could carry them.

It's tragic that this trust is waning today.